easy peasy
sweetie pie

Truly scrumptious treats for kids who love to bake

Mary Contini

EBURY PRESS
LONDON

This book is dedicated to my
mummy and daddy and all the
children who grew up in the
higgledy-piggledy house.

Also by this author: *Easy Peasy*, Mary Contini and Pru Irvine,
ISBN 0 09 186840 8

First published in 2000

3 5 7 9 10 8 6 4 2

First published in the United Kingdom in 2000 by Ebury Press
Random House, 20 Vauxhall Bridge Road, London SW1V 2SA

www.randomhouse.co.uk

Random House Australia (Pty) Limited
20 Alfred Street, Milsons Point, Sydney,
New South Wales 2061, Australia

Random House New Zealand Limited
18 Poland Road, Glenfield, Auckland 10, New Zealand

Random House South Africa (Pty) Limited
Endulini, 5a Jubilee Road, Parktown 2193, South Africa

The Random House Group Limited Reg. No. 954009

Papers used by Ebury Press are natural, recyclable products made from
wood grown in sustainable forests.

A CIP catalogue record for this book is available from the British Library.

ISBN 0 09 187787 3

Designed by Redpath
Edited by Nicky Thompson
Food photography by Philip Webb
Techniques photography by Creative Photography
Food styling by Dagmar Vasely
Styling by Helen Trent

Printed and bound in Portugal by Printer Portuguesa

Contents

The higgeldy – piggeldy house

A long time ago, maybe even before you were born, there was a higgeldy-piggeldy house.

To reach it, you had to climb up a higgeldy-piggeldy staircase because the house sat on top of a sweetie shop. It looked as if it might slide right off. The sweetie shop was packed from floor to ceiling with jars and boxes and packets of all kinds of fantastic toffees and jellies and chocolates. At the back, there was an ice-cream factory. It had an extraordinarily huge, gleaming pot which made ice-cream all day long. The delicious smell of vanilla and sugar and hot cream wafted through the sweetie shop, through the door and out into the nostrils of all the passers by. They sniffed the air and, without another thought, went inside to buy the most scrumptious ice-cream they had ever tasted.

Inside the house there lived eight children. They were higgeldy-piggeldy children. The oldest boy was very clever and very good. He read and wrote and counted and divided, and did all the things that very clever, very good boys do. There were three higgeldy-piggeldy girls, who weren't really the same, and didn't really like the same things, but they always wore the same clothes and always played with the same toys. They liked to cook and bake and help in the kitchen and spent lots of time making delicious things for all the children to eat.

There were also three extremely excitable, extremely noisy, higgeldy-piggeldy boys. They were all very nearly the same size and the same age. They always had the wrong socks on and never looked tidy. They liked cooking too, but never seemed to have enough time. They climbed and screeched and fought and shouted all day long. They broke lights and tables and chairs and vases, and made the house more higgeldy-piggeldy than ever before.

Oh, and I nearly forgot, there was another little girl. She had big brown eyes and pink cheeks and the longest, thickest plait you have ever seen. (No one had ever had any time to cut it!) She played with all the children and they all played with her! They dressed her and painted her face and threw her up into the air. She was a sweetie pie.

The higgeldy-piggeldy children were always hungry and they loved to eat. They loved their breakfast of toast and fruit and milk. They scoffed their lunch of soup and bread and cheese. They adored their supper of pasta and pizza and salad and their pudding of cakes and custard. And they especially loved ice-cream.

When they were very good and had eaten all their lunch, they were allowed to go down to the sweetie shop underneath the higgeldy-piggeldy house. They went into the ice-cream factory and watched the cream and milk and butter and vanilla being poured into the giant pot. They saw it being chilled and churned, and twirled and mixed until it became the best ice-cream in the world. Then they would pile it onto cones and make the higgeldy-piggeldiest ices you ever did see.

At night-time they were very tired and shockingly grubby. They all queued up for a wash in the huge metal tub that sat in front of a roaring fire and then, cleaned and scrubbed, they would tumble happily into their beds and fall fast asleep.

One night, long after they went to bed, the little girl woke up. She was hungry. She went to tell mother, but mother was sound asleep. She went to tell father. But father was slumped in his chair, snoring as loud as a grumpy bear. So she went to tell the higgeldy-piggeldy children. She told the three boys, but they didn't know what to do. She told the three girls, but they couldn't help. 'I'm hungry', she told the very good, very clever boy. 'I know', he said, with a very clever voice. 'Let's have a midnight feast.'

So they all quietly sneaked past the sleeping mother, past the snoring father and tiptoed into the kitchen. They pulled out the baking book and the flour and the sugar and the eggs. They busily set to work and whisked and sifted and folded and, in no time at all, they made cakes and cookies, Flip Flops and Pixie's Burps. They whizzed shakes and slushes and ices and floats. Then, without a word, not even a giggle, they tiptoed back to their bedroom and enjoyed a magnificent, extraordinarily exquisite, higgeldy-piggeldy feast.

And that night, the people in the street looked up surprised as they passed, because the higgeldy-piggledy house was quieter than normal and seemed to be smiling and burping contentedly in the moonlight.

Let's Get Cracking!

Dear Easy peasies

Don't you think it would be great to learn to bake? To be able to make all the cakes and biscuits and the fruity drinks that you like? If you're anything like me, you'll love cakes and cookies. But I'll tell you something: when you make them yourself, they taste even better. You'll be amazed how easy it is.

I know lots of adults who say they can't bake. Well, don't tell them, but it really *is* Easy Peasy. Your sports teacher will be impressed with your knowledge of body-building drinks. Your maths teacher will wonder why you are so good at measuring and weighing. And your friends will be desperate to know how you make your own popcorn.

There's just one thing you should remember – P.M.P. Practice Makes Perfect. If you don't get it quite right the first time, don't worry. The next time, it'll be much easier. Keep baking. If you practise often, you'll end up only checking the book for ideas and quantities. And don't forget to keep notes when you're baking. Perhaps your oven temperature was a bit high. You hated the nuts. You liked different fruit. You'll see, before you can say 'whisk an egg', you'll be making your very own Easy Peasy recipes.

Have fun!

Lots of love

Mary x x x

who wants to Help?

Dear Grown-ups

Do you remember the first time you made fairy cakes? Or you may never have baked a cake in your life but wish you could. Cooking is a life skill; children love it and should learn as early as possible. You'll be absolutely amazed how quickly they learn, and how skilled they become. You'll be surprised at how much they can manage on their own so, except for the recipes which ask you to help, please just keep an eye on things and let them get on with it. Put your feet up and have a rest.

And what about their diet? They may be making biscuits and cakes but I think that baking and making delicious drinks and treats can be a great incentive to get kids into the kitchen. After that, it will be a natural progression to start cooking other things. We all need treats now and then, and a little of this and that does you more than good. And let's face it, if they're normal kids, they'll be scoffing chocolate and crisps and spurious concoctions of sugared drinks throughout the day anyway. So let's get them cooking their own treats and learning what goes into them. Kids are thinkers and giving them knowledge will help them make decisions about what they choose to eat, and when they eat it.

And if they make a dreadful mess, who cares! That's what soap and water are for.

Let them bake cake!

Love

Mary x

How to be a Brilliant Baker

Baking Tray

Always give a baking tray a **good greasing** with soft butter or oil. This stops things sticking. You should also line it with a piece of **non-stick parchment** paper. Lots of things **spread** when they cook, so space things well out on the tray to give them plenty of room.

Beating

Before you start whisking and whirling, find out about the mixer you have in your kitchen. If it is a **free-standing electric mixer** you can stop and start the mixing while you add each ingredient. It makes things quite easy, but sometimes you can't see what's going on. It usually has a bowl specially to go with it and an attachment for whisking and another one for beating.

In the recipes in this book, we use a **hand-held electric blender** (see page 11). It is quite good because once you learn how to use it you can control the stages more easily and see what is happening clearly. You may need to tip the bowl so that the beaters are completely in the mixture. Putting a damp tea towel under the mixing bowl will stop it sliding about.

You can even beat a cake with a **wooden spoon** or a **metal balloon whisk**, but it takes a lot, lot longer. Whatever you use, always make sure that the butter or margarine is **nice and soft**, otherwise it is very difficult to blend things together. Get an adult to help you when you start, then after that it's Easy Peasy.

Boiling

This just means liquid that's hot enough to **bubble** fast.

Brushing

Painting the top of scones and tarts with a little beaten egg or milk makes them **shiny**. Brushing a little beaten egg or milk between two bits of pastry will help them **stick** together.

Burning

If the oven was too hot or you leave a cake in it for too long, the cake will **burn**. Always set the timer when you put things into the oven. If something burns, cook it less next time. Make a note in your book to remind yourself.

Cooling

When things come out of the oven, let them cool for a **few minutes**. After that you can turn them out onto a **wire cooling rack** to cool completely.

Creaming

When you beat soft butter and sugar together they get **very pale and light and creamy**. This is called creaming and takes a bit of time. **Be patient**. When you add eggs, the mixture becomes even **paler, creamier and almost doubled in size**.

Curdled

If you beat cream too much it curdles and gets **lumpy and watery** – yuck! If you curdle cream you will have to throw it away. When you add eggs to creamed butter and sugar they can curdle. Adding a tablespoon of flour stops this happening.

Folding

Use a **big metal spoon** to fold flour or whisked eggs into a mixture. This helps to keep **air** in the mixture so it stays **light and fluffy**. Remember to push the spoon down to the **bottom of the bowl** to mix everything properly.

Food Processor

This is not always the easiest tool to use for baking. It's better to use a hand-held electric blender, a free-standing mixer or even a wooden spoon.

Grating

A grater is used to shred foods. Be very careful not to **grate your fingers**. Ouch!

Greasing and Lining Tins

Greasing baking tins with soft butter or margarine stops cakes **sticking**. Always line a tin with non-stick baking parchment or greaseproof paper as well. This is a **bit of a bore**. You can buy **ready-cut tin liners** which are brilliant! Otherwise you will have to trace out the shape of the tin with a pencil and cut out the right-sized piece with scissors.

Hands

Hands have a nasty habit of getting **sticky** when you are baking. Always start with **clean** hands and nails. Dusting your hands with **a little flour** stops things sticking to them.

Hand-held Electric Blender

Using a hand-held electric blender is the easiest way to get things mixed and creamy. Get an **adult to help** you the first time you use one. Use a big bowl and put a damp clean tea towel underneath it to stop it slipping. Start with the **slowest speed** and work up. Don't switch the mixer on until it is in the middle of the mixture otherwise you will need to **redecorate the kitchen**. Always switch it off **before** you take it out of the mixture. **NEVER** work with **wet hands** or use it near the sink (see Beating on page 9).

Is it Cooked?

When a cake is cooked it will be **springy** when you press it in the middle. If you push a metal **skewer** into the middle of the cake it comes out clean when the cake is cooked. If it doesn't, put the cake back into the oven for another 5 minutes. Then test it with the skewer again.

Kettle

Always use **hot water** from the kettle, not from the tap or the bath. Be very careful not to leave the **flex** hanging over the edge of the worktop.

Liquidising

Liquidising is a great big word for making things **smooth**. Pile things you want to blend into the liquidiser but don't fill it too full. Remember to put the **lid on** unless you want to **terrify the cat**! Sometimes things get stuck. Switch the liquidiser off and push the contents down with a wooden spoon. Never take the lid off while it is whizzing unless you want to look like a **batter-splashed clown!**

Look and Learn

You may not want to hear this, but baking is very like **science**. Look at the mixture when you are working through the stages and watch how it changes. Oh, and by the way, you can eat the experiment – which you can't do in science!

Measuring

Do you want to know a **secret**? Recipes work much better when you weigh things exactly. Ask an adult to explain how your weighing scales work – they're all different. Measure liquid in a measuring jug. Look at the level of the liquid directly against the markings on the jug to measure accurately.

Melting

This means to heat something very **slowly** until all the solid bits become liquid or dissolve.

Notes

You won't remember how long something took to cook, who really liked it or if you would have preferred it with more fruit or less sugar. Keep a note about recipes you try if you want to change things next time.

Ovens

Here's a tricky one! **Every oven is different**. Usually an oven is hotter on the top shelf than the bottom. If the oven has a fan, the heat will be even all over. Ask an adult to explain what type of oven you have. Think of the oven as a **source of heat**. Set the temperature as explained in the recipe. Use the shelf suggested. Set the **timer** and then **leave things alone**. The more you bake in your oven the more you will understand how it relates to the expected cooking times in the recipe. Keep a note if something took a lot longer or shorter to cook.

	°C	°F	gas mark
COOL	120-140	250-275	½-1
good for meringues and pavlova			
MEDIUM	170-180	325-350	3-4
good for small cakes and buns			
QUITE HOT	190-200	375-400	5-6
good for cakes, pastry and biscuits			
HOT	220-230	425-450	7-8
good for choux pastry (Pixie's Burps)			

Oven Gloves

Unless you want to cry and weep, always use them when you are handling anything hot.

Oven Shelves

It's a good idea to check that the oven shelves are in the correct position **before** you switch the oven on. Check that the baking tray or baking tin that you are using fits into the oven.

Ovenproof

An ovenproof dish is one that can be put into a hot oven and will not crack. Once it has cooled down, soak it in soapy water so it is easier to clean.

Piping

You can decorate cakes with pretty rosettes and twirls by squeezing whipped cream or icing out of the nozzle of a piping (squirting) bag (see page 116).

Risen

When a cake rises, it is higher and fuller than when it was put into the oven. This is a good sign that it is cooked.

Rolling

Make sure the work surface is **clean**. Dust it and the rolling pin with a little **extra flour** to stop things sticking. Don't press too hard. Keep moving the pastry round so that you roll it out **evenly**.

Rubbing In

Rubbing butter and flour together between your fingers and thumbs makes them combine and look like **breadcrumbs**.

Separating Eggs

My favourite party trick. Always have 3 small bowls ready – one for the separated whites, one for the yellow yolks and the third to use for each egg you separate. Give the egg a **good whack** in the middle on the side of the bowl. Hold the egg **upright** in one hand, push your thumb into the crack and gently prise apart the shell, keeping the **yellow yolk** safely inside. Let the egg **white drip** into the bowl. Now, gently tip the yolk into the other half of the shell and more white will drip into the bowl. Keep going until you have got rid of most of the white. Pop the yolk into another bowl which you can use to keep all the yolks. **Check the whites**. If there is even a smidgen of yolk they will never whisk to make meringues.

Sifting

A sieve is a fine mesh which is used to take lumps out of flour or icing sugar. When you put the flour or sugar into the sieve, over a bowl, it starts to fall out right away. Hold the sieve a little above the bowl and lightly tap the side. Sifting flour also adds some **air** into it to make your baking light.

Simmering

Liquid that simmers is just hot enough to bubble **gently** on a very low heat.

Soft Peak Stage

Think of the high peaks of the mountains in the Alps, spiky and white with snow, and imagine that they are made of cream or meringue. That's what we call soft peak stage when cream or egg whites are being whisked.

Spatula

Use a spatula to **scrape** out the sides of the baking bowl. If there are raw eggs in the mixture **don't lick** the spatula...there are sometimes **nasty bugs** in raw eggs.

Steaming

This is just cooking food slowly in the steam of boiling water.

Storing

Always store cakes and biscuits separately in tins with a **tight lid**. Don't store them until they are completely **cold**.

Tablespoons and Teaspoons

Use a level tablespoon or teaspoon when you are measuring, unless the recipe says it should be rounded or heaped. (A tablespoon is a soup spoon.)

Teeth

I've still got mine. It's a nuisance, but teeth prefer sweet food **after a meal** and...they like to be brushed twice a day, just like your hair!

Timer

Good for getting you out of **bed** in the morning. Also good for timing things in the oven so that you don't open the oven door too soon...or too late and end up with burnt offerings.

Tin Sizes

The baking tin sizes in the recipes are a good guide. Use the **nearest** you have in your kitchen, but stick to the same shape. If the tin is a **lot smaller** the cake won't have enough room to rise. If it is a **lot bigger** it will not rise at all.

Whipping

Mixing something very fast until it gets **big and fluffy**. Whipping makes cream stiff or eggs double in size. You can use a balloon whisk or a hand-held electric blender. Whipping too much can curdle and spoil cream: a **minor disaster**.

Zester

The zest of an orange or lemon is the outer, coloured skin. The white bitter **flabby** bit underneath is the pith. It doesn't taste so good. Always **wash** the fruit well in hot water before you take the zest off. Pull the zester firmly over the skin to remove the zest – a bit like **grazing** your knee.

Shop 'till you Drop – Baking Things

Lots of baking ingredients are tucked away in drawers and cupboards in the kitchen. Make sure you use the exact ingredient that the recipe asks for. Check the date code on the packet. If it's been lying around for 1000 years it won't be any good.

Air

This is one of the most important ingredients in baking. No, don't blow on all your cakes, but always sift flour and stir your mixtures lightly.

Baking Parchment

This is special paper for lining baking tins. It does not burn in the oven and stops things sticking. Greaseproof paper works as well.

Baking Powder

This is used in small quantities to make cakes and biscuits lighter. When it is added, it **burps** little bubbles of carbon dioxide which get trapped in the cake and make it light.

Bicarbonate of Soda

This is **another burping** powder but has quite a sharp taste and only works in certain recipes. Don't use the wrong one.

Butter or Margarine

If you can, use **unsalted** butter for baking. Margarine works as well but doesn't give such a creamy taste. Low-fat margarine is too watery and won't make good cakes. Butter is **chilled** when it comes straight out of the fridge (so would you be!). **Soft** butter has been out of the fridge for an hour or two and is easier to mix with.

Chocolate

Chocolate can be **sweet** or **bitter**. Bitter chocolate is good in baking because it will give a good chocolaty taste. Chocolate drops are good for cookies.

Cocoa Powder

This useful powder gives a chocolate flavour and colour to cakes.

Cream

You can buy **double** or **whipping cream** which both make whipped cream. Single cream has less fat and is good for mixing and baking but won't whip. You can use crème fraîche or soured cream which are slightly **less rich** and a **bit sour**. **Taste** them and see if you like them. **Mascarpone** is the richest, creamiest cream of all. It needs to be mixed with cream because it is too thick.

Custard Powder

An Easy Peasy way to make custard. Don't use too much or the custard will be too thick. Always dissolve the custard powder in a little milk before mixing it in to the milk to stop the custard getting lumpy. Yuck! Custard can also be made with egg yolks and cream but it's a bit tricky. If you have spare egg yolks an adult might want to make custard with them.

Desiccated Coconut

Dried, sweet coconut, nice for adding sweetness to baking.

Dried Fruit

Raisins, sultanas, dates, dried apricots and prunes are lovely chopped up and added to cakes and biscuits. They are all quite sweet but are **packed** with flavour and **vitamins**. Dried fruit often still have the stones inside. You will have to cut them in half and pull out the stone. It is easier to buy **ready-stoned** dried fruit, or better still, ready-chopped dried fruit.

Eggs

If you can, use **large** eggs in these recipes. Eggs make cakes rise and add good flavour. Make sure that the eggs you use are as fresh as possible. It's bad news, but raw eggs sometimes have **nasty little bugs** in them. **Don't lick** bowls and spoons with mixtures with raw eggs in them…Not fair, I know.

Flour

There are all sorts of flour ground from all sorts of grains to use in different cooking. In this book we use **plain flour, self-raising flour** and **cornflour**. Always use the right one and always sift it through a sieve.

Fruit

Fruit is one of the most delicious ingredients in baking and cooking. Things will taste nicer if the fruit is ripe and juicy. Most fruit can easily be peeled with a vegetable peeler. Work on a clean chopping board and be careful not to chop your fingers.

Glacé Cherries

These are the sticky, sugary cherries that look good as a decoration on top of biscuits and cakes.

Jelly

Ready-prepared jelly comes in lots of different flavours. It contains **gelatine** which is the substance that makes things **set**.

Lemons

You can squeeze a lemon with a fork or a juice squeezer. Asking a **passing elephant** to stand on it will also work! Cut the lemon in half with a sharp knife, push a fork into the middle and squeeze out the juice. It will splash, so point it away from your eyes. If you warm a lemon in the oven for 5 minutes beforehand, you get more juice. Pop it in a warm oven or in a microwave for 30 seconds.

Milk

You can use **full-fat** or **semi-skimmed** milk in the recipes. Skimmed milk is a bit too thin and wishy-washy.

Nuts

Nuts add flavour and texture to baking. Some people are **allergic** to nuts, so be very careful. Even things that have been in contact with nuts can cause an allergic reaction. Always **let everyone know** if you are using nuts and remember to **mark the tin** you store the baking in as well. Nuts can go **rancid** and sour when they are old. Taste one before you add them to the mixture to make sure they are OK.

Oats

A grain mainly used to make porridge and bread. Oats have quite a rough texture.

Oil

Use oils with **no flavour** in baking. **Sunflower** or **vegetable oil** is good.

Popping Corn

Dried corn kernels. Good for popping or feeding pigeons.

Salt

A pinch of salt simply means the amount of salt you can hold between your thumb and first finger…it is just a pinch!

Savoiardi Biscuits

Italian, dry biscuits which are a bit like trifle sponges. They are also called boudoir biscuits. They are good for flavouring with fruity or coffee liquid.

Sugar

If you can, use **unrefined** sugar because it has a better taste. Granulated sugar is **rough** and good for toffee. Caster sugar is **smoother** and is good for cakes and meringues. Soft brown sugar has a lovely toffee taste. Icing sugar is **fine and powdery** and is perfect for making smooth icings and for dusting cakes. Always use the same sugar as the one given in the recipe.

Spices

Spices add lots of **smell** and **taste** to baking. They must be **fresh**. Old spices taste like sawdust.

Squirting Cream

Ready-whipped long-life cream comes in a can and is useful to squirt over ice-cream and pancakes. Yum!

Syrup and Treacle

Syrup is sweet, pale and sticky. Treacle is the same texture but is dark and stronger flavoured. They are both very **messy** and come in tins or in easy-to-pour plastic bottles. The easiest way to measure them is by dipping a tablespoon into a mug of **hot water**. The warm spoon can then be used to scoop out the treacle or syrup which will then **slip easily** off. **Maple syrup** comes from the sap of the Canadian maple tree and has a wonderful toffee flavour. It is easy to pour over pancakes or ice-cream.

Vanilla

Best-known for flavouring **ice-cream**, this comes from a vanilla pod. It smells very sweet and adds a lovely rich flavour to things made with eggs, cream or sugar. Vanilla extract is pure, thick liquid squashed from lots of vanilla pods.

Bits and pieces

1

2

3

4

5

6

7

8

9

10

12

15

16

17

18

19

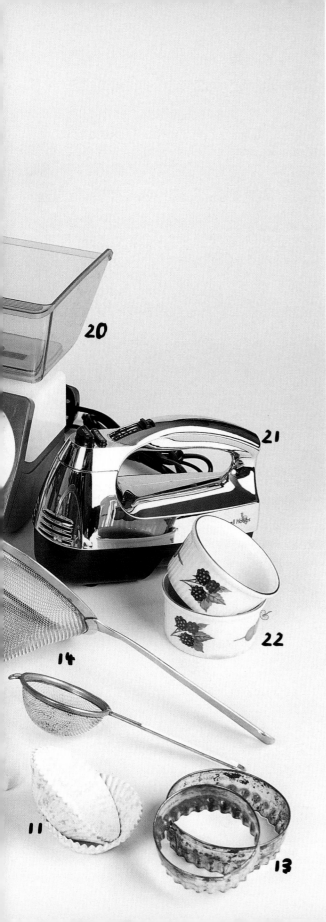

1. grater
2. rolling pin
3. spatula
4. wooden spoons
5. skewer
6. zester
7. vegetable peeler
8. pastry cutter
9. apple corer
10. pastry brushes
11. paper cases
12. tin opener
13. biscuit cutters
14. sieves
15. plastic pudding bowl and lid
16. timer
17. measuring jug
18. liquidiser
19. toothpicks
20. weighing scales
21. hand-held electric blender
22. ramekins

More Bits and Pieces

1. oven glove

2. spatula

3. wooden fork

4. balloon whisk

5. sharp knife

6. fish-slice

7. large metal spoons

8. piping (squirting) bag

9. ice-cube tray

10. wire cooling rack

11. baking tray

12. large mixing bowl

13. apron

14. lined baking tin

15. small bowls

16. ready-cut baking tin liners

17. plastic pudding bowl and lid

18. round baking tin

19. baking parchment

Who wants to Bake a Cake?

Hang on! Before you begin:

- Easy Peasy means **being prepared**. Get everything ready before you start cooking.

- Easy Peasy means **being accurate**. Make very sure that you have the **correct ingredients** and that they are weighed out exactly as in the recipe.

- Easy Peasy means laying all the ingredients out in the **order that they are listed** and counting to make sure that you have everything. Work your way along the ingredients as the recipe tells you and then you won't miss anything out.

- If the recipe tells you to do something you don't understand, look back at the sections on '**How to be a Brilliant Baker**' (see page 9) and '**Bits and Pieces**' (see page 20).

- Remember to **take care** when using sharp knives and always use oven gloves when taking things in and out of the oven.

- Remember to **turn off the oven or cooker** when you have finished cooking.

- Easy Peasy Baking means leaving the kitchen **clean and tidy**.

I Can Bake Cakes

You will need 6 ingredients:

110g of self-raising flour
1 teaspoon of baking powder
2 large eggs
110g of soft margarine
110g of caster sugar
1 tablespoon of milk

weighing scales
a sieve
a tablespoon and a teaspoon
small bowls and a large mixing bowl
a hand-held electric blender
a spatula
a 12-hole muffin tray with a paper case
  in each hole
oven gloves and a timer
a metal skewer
a wire cooling rack

1. Turn on the oven to 180°C/350°F/gas mark 4.
2. Sift the flour and the baking powder into the large mixing bowl.
3. Break the eggs into a small bowl and beat them with a fork.
4. Add the soft margarine, the caster sugar, the eggs and the milk.

Check that all the ingredients are in the mixture.

5. Use the electric hand-held blender to whisk everything together until the mixture is smooth and creamy.
6. Plop half a tablespoon of mixture into each of the paper cases. Divide any extra mixture between them.
7. Using your oven gloves, put the muffin tray onto the middle shelf of the oven. Set the timer for 15 minutes.
8. When the time is up, use your oven gloves to take the tray out of the oven. The cakes will have risen and be golden on top.
9. To check that they are cooked, push a metal skewer into the middle of one of them. If it is cooked the skewer will come out clean. If not, put the tray back into the oven for another 5 minutes.
10. Let the cakes cool for a few minutes before lifting them onto the wire cooling rack.

JUST aS EaSY PEaSY

• When they are cool you can ice the tops of the cakes with Butter Icing (see page 31).
• Cans of ready-to-squirt cream are very easy to use. Cut the top from each cake, squirt on a blob of whipped cream and stick the top back on. Dust with some icing sugar (see page 116).
• You can even use this mixture to make lots of tiny cakes for a birthday treat. Fill 2 trays of mini-muffin paper cases with 2 teaspoons of the mixture. Bake at the same temperature for 10 minutes. Decorate with icing and chocolate buttons.

icing Rink Topping

You will need 2 ingredients:

1 lemon
2 tablespoons of caster sugar

a lemon zester
a small bowl
a sharp knife
a chopping board
a lemon squeezer
a tablespoon

1. Wash the lemon well with hot water.
2. Scrape off the zest with the zester. Put it into a small bowl.
3. Add the caster sugar.
4. Cut the lemon in half and squeeze out a tablespoon of the juice.
5. Add it to the bowl and mix everything together.
6. Pour this lemon icing over the cake while it is still warm. It will soak in and give the cake a lovely, lemony flavour and a crunchy, sugary topping.

JUST as Easy Peasy

• Make the same icing as above with the juice and zest of an orange instead of a lemon.

Can't Go wrong Cake

This recipe is very old and very clever. First you weigh 3 eggs in their shells. Then you weigh out exactly the same weight of soft butter, caster sugar and self-raising flour. Easy Peasy!

You will need 6 ingredients:

3 large eggs in their shells, weighed
the same weight of soft butter
the same weight of caster sugar
the same weight of self-raising flour
1 lemon
2 tablespoons of milk

weighing scales
teaspoons and a tablespoon
small bowls and a large mixing bowl
a sieve
a hand-held electric blender
a large metal spoon
*a sharp knife, a chopping board and a lemon
   squeezer*
a spatula
*a greased and lined 20cm (8 inch) round cake tin
   about 6cm (2½ inches) deep*
oven gloves and a timer
a metal skewer
a wire cooling rack

1. Turn on the oven to 190°C/375°F/gas mark 5.
2. Put the eggs, still in their shells, onto the scales. Weigh them and write down the weight in grams.
3. Weigh out the same amount each of soft butter, caster sugar and self-raising flour.
4. Break the eggs into a small bowl and beat them with a fork.
5. Put the soft butter and the caster sugar into the big mixing bowl and using the hand-held electric blender, beat them until the mixture turns pale, fluffy and creamy.
6. Add half the egg and a tablespoon of flour. Beat everything together.
7. Add the rest of the egg and beat it in.
8. Sift in the rest of the flour and use the large metal spoon to gently fold everything together. Keep the mixture light and fluffy and be careful to mix in all the flour at the bottom of the bowl.
9. Cut the lemon in half and squeeze out a tablespoon of lemon juice.
10. Stir the milk and the lemon juice into the cake mixture.

Check that all the ingredients are in the mixture.

11. Use the spatula to scrape all the mixture into the cake tin, spreading it out evenly.
12. Using the oven gloves, put the cake onto the middle shelf of the oven and set the timer for 35 minutes.
13. When the time is up, use your oven gloves to take the cake out of the oven.
14. Push the metal skewer into the middle of the cake. If it comes out clean the cake is cooked. If not, put the cake back into the oven for another 5 minutes or so.
15. Let the cake cool in the tin for a few minutes before turning it out onto a wire rack.
16. While the cake is still a bit warm add some Icing Rink Topping (see page 27).

Stick to your Teeth Cake

You will need 7 ingredients:

175g of stoned dates
140g of soft brown sugar
85g of butter
175ml of cold water
175g of self-raising flour
1 teaspoon of bicarbonate of soda
2 eggs

a sharp knife and a chopping board
weighing scales
a measuring jug
a small saucepan
some spoons and a fork
small bowls and a large mixing bowl
a sieve
a wooden spoon
a spatula
a greased and lined baking tray about 31cm long,
   21cm wide and 4cm deep (12 x 8 x 1½ inches)
oven gloves and a timer
a metal skewer

1. Turn on the oven to 180°C/350°F/gas mark 4.
2. Chop the dates carefully using the sharp knife.
3. Put the soft brown sugar, the butter and the water into the small saucepan and heat it gently until everything has melted.
4. Take the saucepan off the heat and stir in the chopped dates.
5. Sift the flour and bicarbonate of soda into the large mixing bowl.
6. Pour the liquid mixture into the flour.
7. Break the eggs into a small bowl and beat them with a fork. Add them to the large bowl.
8. Mix everything together with a wooden spoon, making sure that all the flour at the bottom is mixed in. The mixture is quite gloopy.

Check that all the ingredients are in the mixture.

9. Use the spatula to scrape the mixture into the prepared baking tray.
10. Using your oven gloves, put the tray onto the middle shelf of the oven. Set the timer for 25 minutes.
11. When the time is up, use your oven gloves to take the tray out of the oven.
12. Check that the cake is cooked by pushing the metal skewer into the middle. If it comes out clean it is cooked. If not, pop it back into the oven for another 5 minutes.
13. Serve squares of the cake warm with Hop Scotch Sauce poured over it.

Hop Scotch Sauce

You will need 3 ingredients:

125g of butter
175g of soft brown sugar
150ml of double cream

weighing scales
a measuring jug
a small saucepan
a wooden spoon

1. Put the butter, the soft brown sugar and the double cream into the small saucepan.
2. Let it melt slowly over a low heat.
3. Stir everything together to make a smooth sauce.
4. Pour the hot sauce over squares of Stick to Your Teeth Cake.

JUST AS EASY PEASY

• This sauce is yummy poured hot over ice-cream or over Flip Flops (see page 56).

Butter Cream Topping

You will need 3 ingredients:

100g of soft butter
300g of low-fat smooth soft cream cheese
150g of icing sugar

weighing scales
small bowls and a large mixing bowl
a sieve
a fork
a teaspoon
a mug of hot water and a knife

1. Mix the soft butter and low-fat cream cheese together in the mixing bowl.
2. Sift the icing sugar into the large mixing bowl.
3. Mix everything together with the fork. The icing sugar will splash about a bit.
4. Add a teaspoon of cold water if the mixture is too stiff and hard.
5. This is delicious on Honey Bunnies (see page 34). Dip the knife into the mug of hot water and then use it to spread a little Butter Cream Topping onto each Honey Bunny. The hot, wet knife makes the icing easier to spread and leaves it nice and glossy.

JUST AS EASY PEASY

• You can make a Butter Icing with 50g of soft butter, 100g of icing sugar and 2 teaspoons of warm water. Just beat the butter until it is soft and creamy, then mix in the icing sugar and enough water to make a thick, smooth icing.

whipped Cream

*Double cream or whipping cream can be whipped into lovely soft folds by whisking air into it. You can do this quickly with a hand-held electric blender or more slowly with a balloon whisk. It can be a bit tricky. If the cream is whipped too much it will **curdle** and spoil. The secret is to beat it very **slowly** and, as soon as it starts to thicken, be **very careful** not to beat it too much.*

You will need 2 ingredients:

a medium carton of double cream (about 170ml)
2 teaspoons of caster sugar

a large mixing bowl
a hand-held electric blender or a balloon whisk
a teaspoon
a spatula

1. Pour the cream into the large mixing bowl.
2. Add the sugar.
3. Using the hand-held electric blender or the balloon whisk, start to beat the cream. It will gradually thicken, and then start to fluff up.
4. As you see it thicken, whip it a little more slowly until it looks like big soft folds.
5. Use the teaspoon or spatula to transfer the cream onto whatever you have baked. Or use a squirting bag (see page 116) to pipe creamy decorations.

JUST aS eaSY PEaSY

• Make coffee-flavoured whipped cream by mixing in 2 teaspoons of strong coffee after the cream is whipped.
• Make raspberry ripple cream by swirling 2 teaspoons of raspberry jam into the cream after it is whipped.

Make a fool for yourself

You will need 3 ingredients:

4 tablespoons of raspberries
1 medium carton of double cream lightly whipped
   (see opposite)
1 tablespoon of icing sugar

a tablespoon
a small bowl
a fork
2 serving glasses

1. Rinse the raspberries and throw away any mouldy bits and stalks.
2. Put the cleaned berries into a small bowl and squash them with the fork. Add the icing sugar and mix.
3. Add them to the lightly whipped cream and fold everything together.
4. Divide the fool between the 2 serving glasses.

JUST AS EASY PEASY

• Mix 2 tablespoons of crushed meringues into the fool to make a Cream Mess. Very tasty!
• Make a fool with mashed banana (instead of raspberries) folded into the cream.

Honey Bunnies

You will need 8 ingredients:

115g of grated carrots
150ml of sunflower oil
100g of soft brown sugar
2 large eggs
225g of plain flour
1 teaspoon of baking powder
a pinch of salt
1 teaspoon of ground cinnamon

a vegetable peeler
a sharp knife and a grater
weighing scales
some small bowls and a large mixing bowl
teaspoons and tablespoons
a sieve
a hand-held electric blender
a large metal spoon
a spatula
*a 12-hole muffin tray with a paper case in each
   hole*
oven gloves and a timer
a wire cooling rack

1. Turn on the oven to 180°C/350°F/gas mark 4.
2. Peel the carrots with the vegetable peeler,
grate them and weigh out 115g.
3. Put the sunflower oil, the sugar and the eggs
into the large mixing bowl. Beat everything
together with the hand-held blender.
4. Sift the flour and the baking powder into the
mixing bowl.
5. Add a pinch of salt and the teaspoon of
cinnamon.

6. Mix everything together.
7. Add the grated carrots and fold them in with
the large metal spoon.

Check that all the ingredients are in the mixture.

8. Use the tablespoon and the spatula to put a big
blob of the mixture into each paper case in the
muffin tray. Divide the mixture between them.
9. Using your oven gloves, put the muffin tray
onto the middle shelf of the oven. Set the timer
for 25 minutes.
10. When the time is up, use your oven gloves
to take the muffin tray out of the oven.
11. The Honey Bunnies are cooked if they are well
risen and golden brown on top.
12. Let them cool a little before putting them onto
the wire cooling rack.
13. When they are cool smear them with some
Butter Cream Topping (see page 31).

JUST AS EASY PEASY

• You can make the same mixture with 115g
of grated courgettes instead of the carrots.
I know it sounds a bit odd but, believe me,
they are really good!
• You can add 50g of coarsely chopped walnuts
to make a nutty version.
Don't forget that some people are allergic to nuts.

Witches' Bread and Butter

You will need 10 ingredients:

½ teaspoon of bicarbonate of soda
3 tablespoons of milk
110g of soft butter
110g of soft brown sugar
2 eggs
225g of plain flour
3 tablespoons of treacle
3 tablespoons of golden syrup
1 rounded teaspoon of ground ginger
1 rounded teaspoon of ground cinnamon

weighing scales
a measuring jug
small bowls and a large mixing bowl
tablespoons and teaspoons
a hand-held electric blender
a mug of hot water
a sieve
a spatula
a greased and lined baking tray about 31cm long,
   21cm wide and 4cm deep (12 x 8 x 1½ inches)
oven gloves and a timer
a metal skewer

1. Turn on the oven to 180°C/350°F/gas mark 4.
2. Mix the bicarbonate of soda with the milk in a small bowl.
3. Put the soft butter and sugar into the large mixing bowl and whisk them together with the blender until they become pale, fluffy and creamy.

4. Add the eggs and a tablespoon of flour. Beat everything together.
5. Add the treacle and the syrup. (Dip the tablespoon into the mug of hot water and then into the treacle or syrup. This way the sticky treacle runs off the spoon easily.)
6. Sift the rest of the flour, the ground ginger and the ground cinnamon into the mixing bowl.
7. Add the milk mixture and beat everything together. (This is quite a wet mixture so be careful not to splash everything all over the kitchen!)

Check that all the ingredients are in the mixture.

8. Use the spatula to scrape the gloopy mixture into the greased and lined baking tin.
9. Using your oven gloves, put the baking tin onto the middle shelf of the oven. Set the timer for 1 hour.
10. When the time is up, use your oven gloves to take the tray out of the oven.
11. Push the metal skewer into the middle of the Witches' Bread. If it comes out clean it is cooked. If the skewer still has some soft mixture on it, put the tray back into the oven for another 5 minutes or so.
12. Let it cool in the tray. Cut it into thick slices and spread with plenty of yummy soft butter.
13. When it has cooled, you can wrap the Witches' Bread in tin foil. It will keep for about 2 weeks.

JUST AS EASY PEASY

• Add 2 tablespoons of raisins or sultanas to the mixture.
• Add a tablespoon of chopped stem ginger and another teaspoon of ground ginger if you want to try a spicier taste.

Biscuits and Cookies

Hang on! Before you begin:

- Easy Peasy means **being prepared**. Get everything ready before you start cooking.

- Easy Peasy means **being accurate**. Make very sure that you have the **correct ingredients** and that they are weighed out exactly as in the recipe.

- Easy Peasy means laying all the ingredients out in the **order that they are listed** and counting to make sure that you have everything. Work your way along the ingredients as the recipe tells you and then you won't miss anything out.

- If the recipe tells you to do something you don't understand, look back at the sections on '**How to be a Brilliant Baker**' (see page 9) and '**Bits and Pieces**' (see page 20).

- Remember to **take care** when using sharp knives and always use oven gloves when taking things in and out of the oven.

- Remember to **turn off the oven or cooker** when you have finished cooking.

- Easy Peasy Baking means leaving the kitchen **clean and tidy**.

Giant Chocolate Cookies

You will need 7 ingredients:

125g of soft butter
150g of soft brown sugar
1 large egg
150g of plain flour
½ teaspoon of bicarbonate of soda
150g of chocolate chips
100g of chopped nuts (walnuts or hazelnuts)

weighing scales
small bowls and a large mixing bowl
teaspoons
a hand-held electric blender
a fork
a sieve
a large metal spoon
2 greased and lined baking trays
oven gloves and a timer
a wire cooling rack

1. Turn on the oven to 190ºC/375ºF/gas mark 5.
2. Put the soft butter and sugar into the large mixing bowl and beat them together with the hand-held electric blender until they turn pale, fluffy and creamy.
3. Add the egg and keep beating until the mixture gets paler, fluffier and is almost doubled in size.
4. Sift the flour and the bicarbonate of soda into the mixing bowl.
5. Add the chocolate chips and the chopped nuts and mix everything together with a large metal spoon.

Check that all the ingredients are in the mixture.

6. Put a little flour onto your hands *(clean hands, please!)* to stop them getting sticky. Take about half a tablespoon of the mixture and press it into a round ball.
7. Put the ball of mixture onto one of the greased and lined baking trays. Roll out all the mixture into balls and space them well apart on the trays. They will spread out to about three times their size when they cook.
8. Using your oven gloves, put the trays onto the lowest shelves of the oven. Set the timer for 12 minutes.
9. When the time is up, use your oven gloves to take the cookies out of the oven. If they are cooked they will have spread out and be darker and crisp around the edges. The middles will still be a little soft but will crisp up as they cool.
10. After a few minutes use the spatula to ease them off the paper and onto the wire rack.
11. Once the cookies are completely cooled, store them in an airtight tin.
Don't forget that some people are allergic to nuts.

JUST aS EaSY PEaSY

• Make these nut free by adding an extra 50g of chocolate chips instead of the chopped nuts.
• Leave out the chocolate chips and add 100g chopped ready-to-eat dried apricots, some lemon zest and a teaspoon of ground cinnamon to make yummy golden cinnamon cookies.
• To give a double whammy of chocolate flavour, use only 100g of plain flour and 50g of cocoa powder.

Snack Attack

You will need 5 ingredients:

250g of soft butter
250g of jumbo oats
125g of soft brown sugar
125g of stoned dates
60g of chopped walnuts

weighing scales
a sharp knife and a chopping board
a small saucepan
small bowls and a large mixing bowl
a wooden spoon
a spatula
a greased baking tray, about 31cm long,
  21cm wide and 4cm deep (12 x 8 x 1½ inches)
oven gloves and a timer

1. Turn on the oven to 180°C/350°F/gas mark 4.
2. Using the sharp knife, carefully chop the dates.
3. Put the butter into a small saucepan. Melt it on a low heat on the cooker.
4. Put the oats, the sugar, the chopped dates and chopped walnuts into the large mixing bowl.
5. Add the melted butter and mix everything together with the wooden spoon.

Check that all the ingredients are in the mixture.

6. Use the spatula to scrape the mixture into the greased baking tray. Press everything down with the back of the spoon, to flatten it out evenly.
7. Using your oven gloves, put the baking tray onto the middle shelf of the oven. Set the timer for 20 minutes.
8. When the time is up, use your oven gloves to take the baking tray out of the oven.
9. Let the Snack Attack cool before cutting it into finger-sized pieces. This is really great for school lunch boxes and homework hunger busters.
Remember that some people are allergic to nuts.

JUST AS EASY PEASY

• Put half the mixture into the tray then add a layer of ready-to-eat apricots or a layer of stoned prunes. Put the rest of the mixture on top and bake the same way.

Crunchy Munchies

You will need 8 ingredients:

100g of rolled oats
2 tablespoons of desiccated coconut
1 tablespoon of chopped hazelnuts
1 tablespoon of sunflower seeds
1 tablespoon of sesame seeds
1 tablespoon of runny honey
1 tablespoon of sunflower oil
2 tablespoons of sultanas

weighing scales
small bowls and a large mixing bowl
a greased baking tray (at least 1cm deep)
a tablespoon
oven gloves and a timer
a mug of hot water

1. Turn on the oven to 200ºC/400ºF/gas mark 6.
2. Mix together the oats, coconut, hazelnuts, sunflower and sesame seeds in the large mixing bowl.
3. Dip the tablespoon into the mug of hot water and use this to measure out a tablespoon of runny honey. Pour it over the mixture.
4. Add the tablespoon of sunflower oil. Mix everything together.

Check that you have added all the ingredients.

5. Spread the mixture roughly onto the greased baking tray and, using your oven gloves, put the tray on the middle shelf of the oven. Set the timer for 20 minutes.
6. When the time is up, use your oven gloves to take the tray out of the oven. The mixture will be nicely toasted and chunky.
7. Tip it back into the mixing bowl and add the sultanas. Mix everything together. Leave to cool.
8. Store the Crunchy Munchies in an airtight container. They are really good sprinkled over breakfast cereal, baked fruit or used in Grumpy Angel's Breakfast (see page 50).
Remember that some people are allergic to nuts.

JUST AS EASY PEASY

• Make up Crunchy Munchies with any combination of nuts and dried fruits that you like. You will need to use the oats, honey and oil as a base. Try adding chopped dates, chopped dried apricots, or walnuts and pecans.

Grumpy Angel's Breakfast

If you are a grumpy bear in the morning (just like me!), it probably means that your body needs food and energy after a long sleep. A really yummy energy-packed breakfast will take away all the grumpies and make you into an angel!

You will need:

any mixed fruits such as:
    strawberries, raspberries or blackberries
    a slice of ripe melon
    a kiwi fruit
    an apple
    some grapes
    a peach
6 tablespoons of Greek-style yoghurt
1 tablespoon of Crunchy Munchies (see page 43)

a large mixing bowl
a fork
a vegetable peeler
a sharp knife and a chopping board
some spoons

1. Rinse any soft fruits or berries and throw away the stalks and any mouldy fruit. Put the fruit into the mixing bowl and squash it down with the fork.
2. If you want to, peel the skin off the fruit you are using. If not, just wash the skin well. Chop all the fruit into bite-sized pieces, cutting away any pips or seeds. Put it into the mixing bowl as you go. Prepare as much fruit as you like.
3. Add the yoghurt.
4. Sprinkle a tablespoon of Crunchy Munchies on top.

Stabby Stabby Biscuits

You will need 5 ingredients:

100g of soft butter
50g of caster sugar
120g of plain flour
50g of cornflour
a little extra flour and caster sugar

weighing scales
small bowls and a large mixing bowl
a hand-held electric blender
a sieve
a fork
a rolling pin
a clean work surface, dusted with a little flour
a 5cm (2 inch) round biscuit cutter
2 greased baking trays
oven gloves and a timer
a spatula
a wire cooling rack

1. Turn on the oven to 170°C/325°F/gas mark 3.
2. Put the soft butter and sugar into the mixing bowl and beat them together with the hand-held electric blender until they are very pale and fluffy.
3. Sift the flour and cornflour into the bowl and mix it in with a fork until you get a stiff dough. Dust your hands with a little flour *(clean hands, please!)* and finish pressing the dough together.
4. Use the rolling pin to gently flatten the dough out on the floured work surface. Don't press too hard. Roll the mixture out to about the thickness of a pencil.
5. Use the biscuit cutter to cut small round biscuit shapes.
6. Put the biscuits on the greased baking trays. Collect all the odd pieces of dough left over and press them together. Roll the dough flat again and make the rest of the biscuits. You should get about 24.
7. Stab each biscuit 4 or 5 times with the fork. This stops them puffing up when they are cooking.
8. Using your oven gloves, put the baking trays onto the lowest shelves of the oven. Set the timer for 30 minutes.
9. When the time is up, use your oven gloves to take the biscuits out of the oven. They should be firm when pushed down, but still pale in colour.
10. Allow them to cool for 10 minutes or so before using the spatula to transfer them to the wire cooling rack. Sprinkle them with a little caster sugar.
11. When the biscuits are completely cooled they can be stored in a tight-lidded tin. They will stay fresh for 2-3 weeks.

Jammy Piece

To make 6 you will need 5 ingredients:

100g of icing sugar
1 tablespoon of cold water
12 Stabby Stabby Biscuits
some jam
glacé cherries or jelly sweets to decorate

weighing scales
a sieve
a large mixing bowl
a tablespoon
a knife
a mug of hot water
a serving plate

1. Sift the icing sugar into the bowl.
2. Add the water and mix it to make a stiff icing. It only takes a little water to make the icing, so keep mixing and only add another splash of water if you think the icing is too hard.
3. To make the Jammy Pieces stick 2 Stabby Stabby Biscuits together with a teaspoon of jam.
4. Carefully dip the knife into the mug of hot water and then use it to smear some icing over the top of the biscuits.
5. Make up all the biscuits and put them on a serving plate.
6. Decorate each one with a glacé cherry or a jelly sweet.

Queen of Tarts

You will need:

1 quantity of Stabby Stabby Biscuit dough
  (see page 46)
a little flour
some ready-to-squirt cream or Whipped Cream
  (see page 32)
some strawberries
some strawberry jam

a 12-hole muffin tray
12 paper cases
a clean work surface
a rolling pin
a biscuit cutter about 8cm (3 inches) wide
  (or a mug or glass that wide)
teaspoons
a knife
oven gloves and a timer
a wire cooling rack

1. Make the Stabby Stabby Biscuit dough.
2. Put a paper case into each space on the muffin tray.
3. Sprinkle some flour on the clean work surface and onto the rolling pin. Gently press out the biscuit mixture to the thickness of a pencil. Be careful not to press it too hard or it will stick.
4. Use the biscuit cutter to cut out a round shape. Lift this up and ease it into one of the paper cases in the muffin tray, pressing it slightly around the sides to make a cup shape.

5. Use up all the mixture in this way.
6. Put the tray in the fridge for half an hour or so to chill the pastry. This stops it shrinking when you bake it.
7. Turn on the oven to 150°C/300°F/gas mark 2. Let it heat for 10 minutes or so.
8. Using your oven gloves, put the tray on the bottom shelf of the oven. Set the timer for 30 minutes.
9. When the time is up, use your oven gloves to take the tray out of the oven. Leave the tarts to cool.
10. Wash the strawberries and slice some of them, keeping some nice ones to decorate the tarts with.
11. To make the Queen of Heart Tarts, put a teaspoon of jam at the bottom of each tart. Add a few slices of strawberry and top these with a squirt of cream.
12. Put a big yummy strawberry on the top of each tart.

Just as easy peasy

• You can fill these tarts with any jam and fruit that you like. Try raspberries or blackberries.
• Try filling the bottom with some Toffee Bananas (see page 62) and topping them with a blob of whipped cream.
• Instead of putting the prepared tarts in the fridge to chill before baking them, you can **bake them blind** instead. This means weighing them down with some dried peas or beans so that they keep their shape while they are cooking. Just put a second paper case over the pastry and add a teaspoon of dried peas or beans. After they are cooked and cooled, lift off the pastry case and the peas or beans.

Coconut Kisses

You will need:

145g of soft butter
85g of caster sugar
110g of plain flour and a little extra for dusting
55g of cornflour
55g of desiccated coconut
some glacé cherries to decorate

weighing scales
small bowls and a large mixing bowl
a hand-held electric blender
a sieve
a tablespoon
2 greased and lined baking trays
oven gloves and a timer
a spatula
a wire cooling rack

1. Turn on the oven to 180°C/350°F/gas mark 4.
2. Put the soft butter and sugar into the large mixing bowl and beat them with the hand-held electric blender until the mixture is pale, white and fluffy.
3. Sift the flour and cornflour into the bowl. Add the coconut. Stir everything together with the tablespoon to make a dough. The mixture is quite stiff. You might find it easier to dust your hands with a little flour *(clean hands, please!)* and press the mixture together by hand.

Check that all the ingredients are in the mixture.

4. Take pieces of the mixture and roll them into little balls. Put them onto the greased and lined baking trays. They will spread a little when they cook, so space them well apart.
5. Push a glacé cherry into the middle of each coconut kiss, pressing it down with your finger.
6. Using your oven gloves, put the baking trays onto the lowest shelves of the oven. Set the timer for 20 minutes.
7. The Kisses are cooked when they just start to turn golden brown at the edges. When the time is up, use your oven gloves to take the trays out of the oven. Let the Kisses cool a little on the tray before using the spatula to transfer them to the wire rack.
8. Store them in a tight-lidded tin when they are cool.
9. These are especially nice to give as a present to someone you love!

This is Easy peasy

Hang on! Before you begin:

- Easy Peasy means **being prepared**. Get everything ready before you start cooking.

- Easy Peasy means **being accurate**. Make very sure that you have the **correct ingredients** and that they are weighed out exactly as in the recipe.

- Easy Peasy means laying all the ingredients out in the **order that they are listed** and counting to make sure that you have everything. Work your way along the ingredients as the recipe tells you and then you won't miss anything out.

- If the recipe tells you to do something you don't understand, look back at the sections on '**How to be a Brilliant Baker**' (see page 9) and '**Bits and Pieces**' (see page 20).

- Remember to **take care** when using sharp knives and always use oven gloves when taking things in and out of the oven.

- Remember to **turn off the oven or cooker** when you have finished cooking.

- Easy Peasy Baking means leaving the kitchen **clean and tidy**.

Flora's Flop Flops

You will need 7 ingredients:

225g of self-raising flour
1 teaspoon of bicarbonate of soda
a pinch of salt
1 tablespoon of caster sugar
1 large egg
275ml of semi-skimmed milk
some butter for frying

weighing scales
a sieve
small bowls and a large mixing bowl
tablespoons and teaspoons
a fork
a measuring jug
a balloon whisk
some clingfilm
a non-stick frying pan
a fish-slice
a warm serving dish and a clean tea towel

1. Sift the flour into the large mixing bowl.
2. Add the bicarbonate of soda, a pinch of salt and the sugar and mix everything together.
3. Break the egg into a small bowl and beat it with a fork. Add it to the mixing bowl.
4. Add the milk.
5. Use the balloon whisk to mix everything together to make a thick batter. Don't worry about any lumps – keep mixing and they will disappear.

Check that all the ingredients are in the mixture.

6. Cover the bowl with clingfilm and leave it for half an hour or so.
7. Melt a small blob of butter in the frying pan over a medium heat.
8. When it starts to sizzle, put 3 or 4 tablespoons of the thick batter into the frying pan, spaced well apart.
9. Turn down the heat and cook the Flop Flops for 3-4 minutes until lots of little bubbles appear on the surface and they start to brown underneath.
10. Slide the fish-slice underneath and use the fork to help you carefully flip each one over. Cook them for another 2-3 minutes on the other side until they are golden brown.
11. Put the cooked Flop Flops on the warmed plate and cover them with a clean tea towel. Keep them in a warm place and cook the rest of the batter in the same way.
12. These are very nice eaten still warm with butter and a big blob of jam.

JUST as easy peasy

• Add 2 tablespoons of raisins or 2 tablespoons of blueberries to the batter.

Flip Flops

You **need 5 ingredients:**

100g of plain flour
300ml of semi-skimmed milk
2 large eggs
2 tablespoons of caster sugar
some butter

weighing scales
a sieve
a large bowl
a measuring jug
a liquidiser with a lid
a non-stick frying pan
a tablespoon
a fish-slice and a fork
a warm serving plate and a clean tea towel

1. Sift the flour into the bowl.
2. Put the milk, eggs, sugar and flour into the liquidiser.
3. Put the lid on the liquidiser and whiz the mixture until it is a smooth batter.
4. Switch off the liquidiser and leave the batter for half an hour.

5. Put a small blob of butter in the frying pan over a medium heat on the cooker. Melt it until it starts to sizzle.
6. Put a tablespoon of the batter into the frying pan.
7. Move the pan around a little from side to side to spread the batter out evenly.
8. Lower the heat a little and cook until you start to see little bubbles appear on the top of the mixture and it looks slightly brown on the underneath edges.
9. Slide the fish-slice under the Flip Flop and use the fork to help you flip it over. Cook it for another 2-3 minutes or so on the other side.
10. Slide the Flip Flop pancake onto the warmed serving dish. Cover it with the clean tea towel and keep the plate somewhere warm.
11. Add another small blob of butter to the frying pan and cook the rest of the batter in the same way.

JUST AS EASY PEASY

• Spread the Flip Flop with some cherry jam and put a big squirt of Whipped Cream (see page 32) on top.
• Smear some butter in the Flip Flop with a little of the jam you like best.
• Maple syrup is my favourite, poured over the Flip Flops with a ball of vanilla ice-cream.

NOT SO SWEETIE PIE

• Use the same recipe but leave out the sugar. Add a pinch of salt instead. Use these Flip Flops as wraps and fill them with savoury fillings. Try ham and cream cheese or grated Cheddar.

Granny's Scones

You will need 6 ingredients:

225g of self-raising flour (and a little extra flour to dust)
2 teaspoons of baking powder
1 tablespoon of caster sugar
50g of cold butter
1 large egg
some milk

weighing scales
small bowls and a large mixing bowl
a sieve
a measuring jug
a fork
teaspoons and tablespoons
a knife
a clean work surface
a rolling pin and a 5cm (2 inch) biscuit cutter
a greased baking tray
a pastry brush
oven gloves and a timer
a wire cooling rack

1. Turn on the oven to 220°C/425°F/gas mark 7.
2. Sift the flour and the baking powder into the large mixing bowl.
3. Add the sugar and stir everything together.
4. Cut the cold butter into small cubes and add them to the bowl. Rub the flour and butter together between your thumb and fingers *(clean hands, please!)*. When the mixture is ready it will look like fine breadcrumbs.

5. Break the egg into the measuring jug. Beat it with the fork and add enough milk to make the volume up to 150ml. Add this to the mixture and use a knife to mix everything together to make a soft dough.

Check that you have added all the ingredients.

6. Sprinkle a little flour onto the clean work surface. Put a little flour on your hands and a little more onto the rolling pin.
7. Put the dough onto the work surface and use the rolling pin to very gently flatten it down. It should be about 3cm thick.
8. Dip the biscuit cutter into a little flour and cut out scones from the dough. Press the cutter straight down so that the scones will rise nice and evenly.
9. Put each scone onto the greased baking tray. Space them apart a little.
10. Press all the odd pieces of dough together and flatten it out. Cut out the rest of the scones.
11. Brush each scone with a little milk.
12. Using your oven gloves, put the baking tray onto the top shelf of the oven. Set the timer for 10 minutes.
13. When the time is up, use your oven gloves to take the tray out of the oven. The scones will have risen and be slightly brown on top when they are cooked.
14. Let the Granny's Scones cool a little before putting them onto the wire cooling rack.
15. Eat them with butter and jam.

JUST AS EASY PEASY

• Make fruit scones by adding 50g of raisins or sultanas at the same time as the caster sugar.
• Make cheesy scones by adding 50g of grated cheese and a pinch of salt instead of the sugar.

All American Chunks

You will need 9 ingredients:

1 tablespoon of cocoa powder
5 tablespoons of cold water
85g of butter
2 large eggs
225g of caster sugar
2 tablespoons of chopped nuts
100g of plain flour
1 teaspoon of baking powder
a pinch of salt

weighing scales
small bowls and a large mixing bowl
some tablespoons
a small saucepan
a hand-held electric blender
a sieve
a large metal spoon
a spatula
oven gloves and a timer
a greased and lined baking tray, about 31cm
  long, 21cm wide and 4cm deep (12 x 8 x 1½
  inches)
a knife

1. Turn on the oven to 180°C/350°F/gas mark 4.
2. Tip the cocoa powder, water and butter into the small saucepan. Put it onto the cooker and heat it slowly. Once the butter has melted, take the saucepan off the heat and mix everything together.
3. Break the eggs into the large mixing bowl. Add the sugar.
4. Use the hand-held electric blender to beat them together until they are pale, light and fluffy.
5. Add the melted chocolate mixture and the chopped nuts and mix.
6. Sift the flour and the baking powder into the mixing bowl. Add a pinch of salt and use the large metal spoon to fold everything together.

Check that all the ingredients are in the mixture.

7. Use the spatula to scrape the mixture into the greased and lined baking tray.
8. Using your oven gloves, put the tray onto the middle shelf of the oven. Set the timer for 35 minutes.
9. When the time is up, use your oven gloves to take the tray out of the oven. The All American Chunks are cooked if they are firm in the middle when you press them with your fingers.
10. After a few minutes, use the knife to cut them into squares. Leave them in the tin until they are cooled.
11. You can store All American Chunks in an airtight container for about 2 weeks.
Remember that some people are allergic to nuts.

JUST AS EASY PEASY

• Leave the nuts out of the recipe to make a nut-free version.

Crisp Apple Strudel

You will need 8 ingredients:

a packet of frozen pastry (about 200g)
3 crunchy apples
2 tablespoons of soft brown sugar
2 tablespoons of sultanas
60g of soft butter
1 teaspoon of ground cinnamon
1 egg
a little granulated sugar

a vegetable peeler
a sharp knife
teaspoons, a tablespoon and a fork
small bowls and a large mixing bowl
a small saucepan
a clean work surface
a greased baking tray
oven gloves and a timer
a rolling pin and a little extra flour
a pastry brush

1. Take the pastry out of the freezer about an hour before you want to use it.
2. Peel the apples. Cut them in half and cut out the middle core and the pips. Cut them into little squares, about the size of sugar cubes.
3. Put the apple into the small saucepan with the sugar, sultanas, soft butter and the ground cinnamon. Mix everything together.
4. Put the saucepan onto the cooker and slowly cook the apple mixture over a low heat for about 15 minutes. Then leave it to cool.
5. Turn on the oven to 190ºC/375ºF/gas mark 5.
6. Dust a little flour over the clean work surface and the rolling pin. Roll out the pastry, turning it round as you go to keep it an even thickness.
7. Cut out 6 or so oblongs, about the size of a slice of bread.

8. Put an oblong of pastry onto the greased baking tray. Put a tablespoon of the apple mixture onto one end of the pastry.
9. Fold the rest of the pastry over to make a parcel. Press the edges down to stick them together.
10. Use the sharp knife to make a few slashes on the top of the pastry parcel, just cutting through the top sheet. This helps the steam to escape while the strudel is cooking so that the pastry will be nice and crisp.
11. Make up the rest of the pastry oblongs in this way, dividing the mixture between them. Don't worry if they are a bit higgeldy-piggeldy. I like them that way.
12. Break the egg into a small bowl and beat it with a fork. Brush the top of each pastry parcel with some of the beaten egg. Sprinkle with a little granulated sugar.
13. Using your oven gloves, put the baking tray onto the top shelf of the oven. Set the timer for 20 minutes.
14. When the time is up, use your oven gloves to take the tray out of the oven. The Crisp Apple Strudels will be puffy, crispy, glistening and golden. If they are a bit pale, pop them back into the oven for another 5 minutes.

JUST AS EASY PEASY

• Add a tablespoon of nibbed almonds (tiny almond cubes) to the mixture and sprinkle a few on top of the parcels before putting them in the oven. *Remember that some people are allergic to nuts.*

NOT SO SWEETIE PIE

• Instead of apple, fill the pastry parcels with slices of tomato, some fresh basil leaves, some Mozzarella cheese and a little salt. Bake them in the same way to make Pillowed Pizzas.

Easy Peasy Toffee Bananas

You will need 3 ingredients:

3 ripe bananas
30g of butter
30g of soft brown sugar

weighing scales
a sharp knife
a chopping board
a medium frying pan
a wooden spoon

1. Peel the bananas and slice them lengthways into 4 or 5 chunks.
2. Put the butter and sugar into the frying pan and melt it slowly. Stir everything with the wooden spoon.
3. Once the sugar has all melted, lay the sliced bananas on top.
4. Turn down the heat and slowly cook the bananas.
5. When they look soft, gently turn them over and cook them on the other side for a few minutes.
6. Use these bananas in pancakes or in crumbles or pies. They are very good with hot Yellow Belly Custard (see page 80).

JUST AS EASY PEASY

• Make toffee apples the same way. Slice the apples very thinly and cook them with a little lemon juice in the sugared butter for about 20 minutes.
• Try pineapple. Cut the pineapple into thin slices using a sharp knife. You may need a little help. Cut the tough, spiky skin off and cut out the hard core. Cook the pineapple in the same way as above.

Popcorn

This really is Easy Peasy. Ask an adult to help you the first time you make it.

You will need 3 ingredients:

2 tablespoons of popping corn
a tablespoon of oil
a tablespoon of caster sugar

tablespoons
a very big, heavy saucepan with a good fitting lid
a large bowl

1. Heat the oil in the saucepan (without the lid) until it just starts to smoke a little.
2. Add the popcorn. Be very careful because the oil might splash. Put the lid on tightly.
3. Turn the heat down low and listen.
4. The heat makes the corn kernels turn inside out and fluff up to 4 times their size. You will hear fantastic popping noises for about 5 minutes. Don't take the lid off the saucepan until the popcorn has stopped popping and the heat is turned off.
5. When the popping stops, turn off the heat. Wait for 5 minutes while the popcorn cools down.
6. Open the lid. You'll get a surprise! The 2 table-spoons of popping corn will now fill the whole pot.
7. Tip the popcorn into a large bowl and sprinkle with the tablespoon of caster sugar.

JUST aS EaSY PEaSY

• Instead of sugar add a little salt.
• You can add maple syrup to make sticky popcorn.

Jellies and Fruits

Hang on! Before you begin:

- Easy Peasy means **being prepared**. Get everything ready before you start cooking.

- Easy Peasy means **being accurate**. Make very sure that you have the **correct ingredients** and that they are weighed out exactly as in the recipe.

- Easy Peasy means laying all the ingredients out in the **order that they are listed** and counting to make sure that you have everything. Work your way along the ingredients as the recipe tells you and then you won't miss anything out.

- If the recipe tells you to do something you don't understand, look back at the sections on '**How to be a Brilliant Baker**' (see page 9) and '**Bits and Pieces**' (see page 20).

- Remember to **take care** when using sharp knives and always use oven gloves when taking things in and out of the oven.

- Remember to **turn off the oven or cooker** when you have finished cooking.

- Easy Peasy Baking means leaving the kitchen **clean and tidy**.

Stained Glass Jelly

You will need 8 ingredients:

8 cubes (½ packet) of strawberry jelly
8 cubes (½ packet) of orange jelly
8 cubes (½ packet) of blackcurrant jelly
3 x 275ml of hot water
1 banana
1 small tin of mandarin oranges
about 10 strawberries, plus a few more
    for decoration
ready-to-squirt cream, to decorate

a measuring jug
a kettle
3 small bowls
1 big clear bowl
a wooden spoon
a knife
a chopping board
a tin opener
clingfilm
a spatula

1. Before you start, check the packet to see how much water is needed to make the jelly. It is usually 275ml for half a packet but change this if the jelly you are using needs a different amount. (Ask an adult to help if you don't understand.)

2. Put 275ml of hot water from the kettle into the measuring jug. Add the strawberry jelly cubes. Stir the mixture with the wooden spoon until the cubes have completely dissolved. Carefully pour the hot jelly into one of the bowls.

3. Wash the strawberries and twist off the stalks. Then slice the strawberries and stir them into the jelly. Cover the bowl with some clingfilm.

4. Make up the blackcurrant jelly in the same way. When it has dissolved, pour it into the second bowl. Slice the banana and add it. Cover this bowl with clingfilm too.

5. Now make up the orange jelly in the same way. When it has dissolved, pour it into the third small bowl. Open the tin of mandarin oranges, pour away the juice and add the segments to the orange jelly. Cover with clingfilm.

6. Leave all three bowls of jelly to cool. (You can put them in the fridge once they have cooled down to room temperature.)

7. When the jellies are almost set, but are still very wobbly, take them out of the fridge.

8. Use the spatula to transfer the strawberry jelly into the big clear bowl. Scoop the orange jelly on top of that. Finally, layer the blackcurrant jelly on top of the orange jelly.

9. Cover the bowl and put it back into the fridge until the Stained Glass Jelly has set completely.

10. Decorate the jelly with some squirting cream and some extra sliced strawberries.

JUST AS EASY PEASY

• Make up any combination of jelly and fruit that you like.

Spicy Baked Apple

You will need 5 ingredients:

2 large crisp eating apples
a blob of butter
1 tablespoon of soft brown sugar
1 tablespoon of chopped ready-to-eat apricots
 or raisins
1 teaspoon of mixed spice

a chopping board
a sharp knife
an apple corer
teaspoons and tablespoons
a greased ovenproof baking dish
oven gloves and a timer

1. Turn on the oven to 190°C/375°F/gas mark 5.
2. Wash the apples. Then use the apple corer to core each apple. The easiest way to do this is to put the apple onto the chopping board. Hold the apple with one hand, then push the apple corer right down the centre of the apple. Twist it round. It needs a bit of muscle. *(You may need an adult to help.)* Pull the corer out and the centre of the apple should come out as well. Be careful not to cut yourself. The corer can slip, so watch out.
3. Put the apples onto the greased baking tray.
4. Chop the apricots if you are using them.
5. Push a little butter, sugar and some chopped apricots or raisins down into the centre of each apple. Add layers and pack everything down with your fingers until each apple is filled up.
6. Put a blob of butter and a little sugar on top of each apple and sprinkle with a little mixed spice.
7. Using your oven gloves, put the apples onto the middle shelf of the oven.
8. Set the timer for 30 minutes.
9. When the apples are cooked they will be soft and fluffy inside, oozing with lovely spicy, buttery juices.

JUST as easy peasy

• You can bake pears in the same way. It is easiest to core them from the fat, bottom part upwards. You could also cut them in half, scoop out the core and pack the middle with the butter, sugar and spices. Bake at the same temperature.

Green Salad

You will need a selection of any of the fruit below:

half a ripe melon
2 kiwi fruit
2 green apples
12 lychees
a handful of sweet white seedless grapes
a small tin of pineapple chunks and their juice
1 orange

a chopping board
a sharp knife
a serving bowl
a vegetable peeler
a tin opener
a lemon squeezer
a tablespoon
clingfilm

1. Scoop the seeds from the melon and cut off the skin. Cut the juicy flesh into bite-sized chunks. Put them into the serving bowl.
2. Use the vegetable peeler to peel the skin from the kiwi fruit. Cut each end off and then cut the fruit into round slices or chunks. Put them into the bowl with the melon.
3. If you want to peel the apple use the vegetable peeler. If not, just wash the skin well. Cut the apples into chunks, cutting away any pips and core. Add them to the bowl.
4. Peel the lychees by squashing them between your fingers and cracking the skin. The soft, white lychees will pop out quite easily. Use the knife to cut into each one and ease out the brown stone inside. Add the lychees to the bowl.
5. Wash the seedless grapes and add them too.
6. Open the tin of pineapple chunks. Add them to the serving bowl with 1 or 2 tablespoons of the juice.
7. Squeeze the orange and add the juice to the bowl.
8. Mix everything together. Cover the bowl with clingfilm and chill the Green Salad in the fridge before eating it.

Red Salad

Use ripe strawberries, redcurrants, raspberries and blackberries. Rinse them, throwing away any that are mouldy, and take off all the stalks. Put the fruit into a serving bowl. Peel a peach and a nectarine. Use a sharp knife to cut them into cubes. Add them to the bowl. Sieve 1 or 2 teaspoons of icing sugar into the bowl. Leave it in the fridge to chill for half an hour before eating.

Yellow Salad

Make a Yellow Salad with mixed melon, banana, yellow pears and grapefruit. Mix small scoops of yellow and green melon together. Add slices of banana and pear. Cut a grapefruit in half. Use a sharp knife to cut round the segments of the grapefruit and scoop out the flesh with a teaspoon. Squeeze the juice from the other half of the grapefruit and mix everything together.

Just Oranges

You will need:

5 big oranges

a sharp knife
a chopping board
a serving bowl
a lemon squeezer
clingfilm

1. Cut the top and bottom off 4 of the oranges.
2. Use the sharp knife to carefully cut the skin from one of these oranges, taking away as much white pith as possible. The easiest way to do this is to stand the orange on the chopping board and slice the skin off in sections, cutting down from top to bottom.
3. Turn the orange on its side and cut it into round slices. Take out any pips.
4. Put the slices in the bowl with any juice that has oozed out.
5. Prepare the other 3 oranges in the same way.
6. Squeeze the juice from the fifth orange and pour it over the orange slices.
7. Cover the bowl with clingfilm and chill the oranges in the fridge for a little while before eating them.

He's a Smoothie

*A smoothie is a **very delicious drink** made of any combination of fruit and milk or yoghurt whizzed together until they are smooth. It is packed with energy – perfect if you are in training for football or a sports event.*

You will need 5 ingredients:

a carton of natural yoghurt (about 125ml)
2 tablespoons of frozen or fresh blueberries
   (or raspberries)
a ripe peach or nectarine
1 tablespoon of runny honey
a little milk

a liquidiser with a lid
a spatula
a chopping board
a sharp knife
a tall glass to serve and a chunky straw

1. Put the yoghurt into the liquidiser. You can use the spatula to scrape it all out.
2. Add the blueberries (or raspberries).
3. Peel and chop the peach or nectarine. Put it into the liquidiser.
4. Add the honey.
5. Put on the lid and whiz until everything is smooth. Add a little milk if you want the Smoothie thinner.
6. Drink the Smoothie through a nice fat straw in a long cool glass.

JUST AS SMOOTHIE

• Try a Green Smoothie with 2 kiwi fruit, a banana and a cup of milk whizzed together.
• Try strawberries, peaches and pears, all peeled, chopped and whizzed with yoghurt.
• Mix a tablespoon of cocoa powder, 4 mint leaves, a ball of vanilla ice-cream and a cup of milk to make a Mint Chocolate Smoothie.

Hot Fruit Salad

You will need 6 ingredients:

1 orange
1 banana
1 apple
1-2 tablespoons of soft brown sugar
half a lemon
a blob of butter

a chopping board
a sharp knife
a greased ovenproof dish
a tablespoon
a knife
a fork
oven gloves and a timer

1. Turn on the oven to 190°C/375°F/gas mark 5.
2. First, slice both ends off the orange. Now, very carefully, cut down from top to bottom to take all the skin off. Cut the white, flabby pith away as well.
3. Slice the orange, take out any pips, and put the pieces into the greased ovenproof dish.
4. Add any juice that has seeped out onto the chopping board.
5. Peel the banana and cut it into thick slices. Add them to the dish.
6. Wash the apple. Cut it in half and then into small chunks. Throw away any core or pips. Put the pieces into the dish.
7. Sprinkle the sugar over the fruit. Squirt a little lemon juice by putting a fork into the lemon half and squeezing the juice out. Add a blob of butter.
8. Using your oven gloves, put the baking dish onto the top shelf of the oven.
9. Set the timer for 25 minutes.
10. The fruit will be soft, juicy and very hot. Let it cool down a little before eating it.

Hop, Skip and Jump

You will need:

a large bowl of breakfast cereal with milk,
  every morning
4-5 slices of bread
lunch and dinner with pasta, potatoes or rice
some fish or chicken or beans
plenty of salad, raw vegetables and even some
  cooked ones!
some cheese and milk
plenty of fresh water and some fresh fruit juice
lots of fresh fruit
treats and puddings once or twice a day, after
  meals if possible

strong healthy bones
clear skin
your own teeth
glossy, shiny hair
lots of energy
plenty of sleep

1. Get up nice and early in the morning so that you have time for breakfast. Orange juice squeezed from the real thing is best.
2. Get off to school and keep an apple or a banana in your bag in case of hunger attacks.
3. Eat lunch. Pizza, pasta, soup and bread, or a baked potato. If you can't get good food from school, bring a packed lunch from home.
4. Snack attack... maybe some cheese or some grapes. Or some of your own Snack Attack (see page 42). Fresh fruit drinks, Smoothies (see page 72) and Shakes (see page 102) have lots of energy.
5. Dinner, I bet you're still nice and hungry. Eat it all up! Pudding... Easy Peasy home-made treats are just the thing.

JUST AS EASY PEASY

• Walking to school or the shops (watch out for traffic!).
• Going out for a game of football.
• Getting on your bike and enjoying a ride.
• Going for a swim instead of a shower (just kidding!).
• Joining the netball team.
• Cooking your own food and treats instead of opening ready meals... Easy Peasy!

Fill me up Treats

Hang on! Before you begin:

- Easy Peasy means **being prepared**. Get everything ready before you start cooking.

- Easy Peasy means **being accurate**. Make very sure that you have the **correct ingredients** and that they are weighed out exactly as in the recipe.

- Easy Peasy means laying all the ingredients out in the **order that they are listed** and counting to make sure that you have everything. Work your way along the ingredients as the recipe tells you and then you won't miss anything out.

- If the recipe tells you to do something you don't understand, look back at the sections on '**How to be a Brilliant Baker**' (see page 9) and '**Bits and Pieces**' (see page 20).

- Remember to **take care** when using sharp knives and always use oven gloves when taking things in and out of the oven.

- Remember to **turn off the oven or cooker** when you have finished cooking.

- Easy Peasy Baking means leaving the kitchen **clean and tidy**.

Get Steaming Pud

This is a really Easy Peasy pudding. It just takes a bit of time and care to cook. Ask an adult to help.

You will need 6 ingredients:

100g of soft butter and an extra blob for greasing
100g of caster sugar
2 large eggs
225g of self-raising flour
3 tablespoons of milk
3 tablespoons of strawberry jam

1.2 litre (2 pint) plastic pudding bowl with a lid
a saucepan with a lid, big enough for the pudding bowl to fit into
a measuring jug
weighing scales
small bowls and a large mixing bowl
a hand-held electric blender
a tablespoon
a sieve
a large metal spoon
a spatula
a circle of baking parchment, the size of the pudding bowl lid
oven gloves and a timer
a knife
a small saucepan
a serving plate

1. First, before you do anything, check that the pudding bowl fits easily into the saucepan. Add some cold water, enough to come halfway up the outside of the pudding bowl. Take the bowl out of the saucepan but leave the water in it until later.
2. Grease the pudding bowl well with the extra blob of butter.
3. Put the soft butter and sugar into the mixing bowl and use the blender to beat everything until the mixture becomes pale, fluffy and almost doubled in size.
4. Break one egg and add it to the bowl with a tablespoon of flour. Beat them in.
5. Break the other egg and beat that in too.
6. Now, sift the rest of the flour into the mixture and use the large metal spoon to fold everything together.
7. Finally mix in the milk.

Check that you have added all the ingredients.

8. Using the spatula, put the mixture into the greased bowl. Flatten it down and pop the circle of baking parchment on top. The bowl will only be about three-quarters full, but the pudding will rise as it is steamed.
9. Press the lid onto the pudding bowl and lower it into the saucepan of water.

GET STEAMING

Get an adult to help you. Boiling water and steam can burn badly.

1. Carefully put the saucepan onto the cooker making sure that the handle does not stick out. Put the lid on and turn on the heat.
2. When the water starts to boil, turn the heat down to low and set the timer for 1½ hours. The pudding will cook slowly in the steam from the water.
3. Every half hour or so, carefully check to make sure that there is still plenty of water in the pot. Add a little more hot water if the level is too low.
4. When the time is up, *ask an adult to help you take the pudding out of the saucepan.*
5. Take the lid off the bowl. Peel off the circle of baking parchment. If the pudding is cooked properly, it will have risen up to the top of the bowl and will be light and springy to touch. If it looks sticky and undercooked, steam it for another 20 minutes or so.
6. Put 3 tablespoons of strawberry jam into the small saucepan and melt it slowly over a low heat.

7. *You may need an adult to help you to do this next bit the first time.* Run a knife around the pudding to loosen it from the sides of the bowl.
Put the serving plate on top of the bowl. Using the oven gloves to hold the bowl firmly, turn the pudding upside down and out onto the plate.
8. Carefully pour the melted jam over the pudding.
9. This is most brilliantly delicious with piping hot Yellow Belly Custard poured over it (see page 80).

Yellow Belly Custard

You will need 3 ingredients:

500ml of full-fat milk
2 tablespoons of custard powder
about 2 tablespoons of caster sugar

a measuring jug
a small bowl
tablespoons
a medium saucepan
a long-handled wooden spoon

1. Put the custard powder and 4 tablespoons of the milk into the small bowl. Stir it well to dissolve any lumps.

2. Put the rest of the milk into the saucepan. Warm it slowly. *Don't leave milk heating on the cooker. When it boils it rises very quickly to the surface and can spill over.*

3. As the milk starts to steam, add the custard mixture. Stir with the wooden spoon until the custard thickens and starts to boil. Don't stop stirring or the custard will get lumpy.

4. Add the sugar. Taste the Yellow Belly Custard (but be careful because it'll be hot!) and add a little more sugar if you like.

JUST AS EASY PEASY

• Make the custard thicker by adding more custard powder. Always dissolve the powder in a little milk before adding it.

• If you need cold custard for a trifle, make the custard with 3 tablespoons of powder and use single cream instead of milk. Cover the Yellow Belly Custard with clingfilm to stop a skin forming on the surface and leave it to cool before putting it into the fridge.

Brumble Grumble

Picking blackberries is great fun. Just remember not to eat them all before you get home.

You will need 8 ingredients:

about 400g of blackberries
about 400g of juicy ripe plums
some soft brown sugar
40g of plain flour
60g of rolled oats
50g of soft brown sugar
100g of cold butter
some cold water

a chopping board
a knife
weighing scales
an ovenproof baking dish, greased with plenty
*   of butter*
a tablespoon
a large mixing bowl
a sieve
oven gloves and a timer

1. Check the blackberries for leaves and caterpillars! Give them a little rinse under cold water and pop them into the bottom of the ovenproof baking dish.
2. Wash the plums. Cut them into quarters and push out the stones. Add the plums to the dish.
3. Mix the fruit together and sprinkle it with the soft brown sugar. Taste to check if it is sweet enough. Add a little more sugar if you like.
4. Turn on the oven to 200ºC/400ºF/gas mark 6.
5. Sift the flour into the large mixing bowl. Add the oats and the sugar and stir everything together.
6. Cut the cold butter into cubes and put it into the bowl. Using your fingers *(clean hands, please!)* rub everything together until the mixture looks like breadcrumbs.
7. Using the spoon, spread the topping roughly over the fruit.
8. Splash the topping with a tablespoon of cold water.
9. Using your oven gloves, put the dish on the middle shelf of the oven. Set the timer for 40 minutes.
10. The Brumble Grumble is cooked when the juice from the fruit seeps through the topping and smells toffee-ish and sweet.

JUST as easy peasy

• Try Brumble Grumble with a big blob of crème fraîche. This is very like cream, but a little bit sour. It tastes very nice with the sweet fruit.
• Make a Grumble with any fruit you like. Try strawberries and banana or peaches and apricots.
• In the spring, some people have rhubarb growing in their gardens. Use about 700g of rhubarb sprinkled with about 6 tablespoons of soft brown sugar to make a Rumble Grumble.

Spice Rice

To start with you will need 2 ingredients:

2 tablespoons of pudding rice
a mug of milk

a tablespoon
a mug
a small saucepan
a wooden spoon

1. Put the pudding rice and the mug of milk into the small saucepan.
2. Put the saucepan onto a low heat on the cooker and stir everything slowly until the milk starts to boil. *Never leave milk on the cooker because it can very easily rise up the sides of the saucepan and boil over.*
3. Let the rice cook slowly for about 10 minutes. Switch off the heat.

Now you will need 5 more ingredients:

400ml of milk
2 large eggs
2-3 tablespoons of caster sugar
some butter
1 pinch of ground cinnamon

a measuring jug
tablespoons and teaspoons
a fork
an ovenproof bowl that holds about 850ml
  (1½ pints), well greased with butter

1. Turn on the oven to 150ºC/300ºF/gas mark 2.
2. Break the eggs into the ovenproof bowl. Add the sugar and beat them together with the fork for a few minutes.
3. Pour in the rice from the small saucepan, add the rest of the milk and mix everything together.
4. Add a few blobs of butter to the top of the rice and sprinkle it with a pinch of ground cinnamon.

Check that you have added all the ingredients.

5. Using the oven gloves, put the bowl of Spice Rice onto the middle shelf of the oven.
6. Set the timer for 45 minutes.
7. When the time is up, use your oven gloves to take the hot pudding out of the oven. Very nice Spice Rice!

JUST AS EASY PEASY

• Add 2 tablespoons of sultanas to the mix before it goes into the oven.
• Add a layer of peeled and sliced (or chopped) peaches to the bottom of the bowl before you add the rice and milk mixture.

wobbly Caramel pudding

You will need 5 ingredients:

2 large eggs
2 tablespoons of caster sugar
300ml of full-fat milk
a blob of butter for greasing the ramekins
some maple syrup

kitchen paper
4 ovenproof ramekins
a measuring jug
a large mixing bowl
a fork
tablespoons
a ladle
a large deep baking tray
a kettle with boiling water
oven gloves and a timer
4 pudding plates and a knife

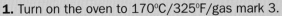

1. Turn on the oven to 170°C/325°F/gas mark 3.
2. Use a piece of kitchen paper and the blob of butter to grease the ramekins well.
3. Break the eggs into the mixing bowl.
4. Add the sugar and mix them together with the fork.
5. Mix in the milk and stir.
6. Use the ladle to divide the egg mixture into the 4 ramekins.
7. Put them into the deep baking tray. *Ask an adult to pour boiling water halfway up the sides of the ramekins and put the tray into the oven.*
8. Set the timer for 45 minutes.
9. *Ask an adult to take the tray out of the oven.*
10. Using your oven gloves to hold the hot ramekin, carefully run a knife around the inside of each one to loosen the pudding.
11. Put a pudding plate over the top of the ramekin and, wearing oven gloves to hold the sides, turn the pudding out onto the plate. *Ask an adult to help you turn it if you find this a bit tricky.*
12. Pour a tablespoonful or so of maple syrup over each Wobbly Caramel Pudding.

Sweetie pie pastry

You will need 5 ingredients:

240g of self-raising flour and a little extra flour
90g of caster sugar
120g of cold butter
1 egg yolk
1 tablespoon of cold water

weighing scales
a sieve
tablespoons
small bowls and a large mixing bowl
a rolling pin
a knife
clingfilm

1. Sift the flour into the large mixing bowl.
2. Add the sugar and mix it in.
butter into small cubes and add it to the
ur fingers *(clean hands, please!)* to rub
ito the flour mixture. Keep rubbing the
and butter between your thumb and fingers,
lifting it up and letting it fall back into the bowl. Keep
doing this until it looks like coarse breadcrumbs.
4. Mix the egg yolk into the mixture with the knife.
5. Add the tablespoon of cold water. Now, dust your
hands with a little flour and press the pastry
together until it forms a ball. It will take a few
minutes to do this. Keep pressing.

Check that all the ingredients are in the mixture.

Apple Filling Station

You will need 3 ingredients:

about 800g of cooking apples or sharp and tasty
   eating apples (about 5 or 6)
2-3 tablespoons of caster sugar
2 tablespoons of cold water

a vegetable peeler
a knife
a chopping board
a small saucepan
a tablespoon

1. Peel the skin from the apples, cut them into quarters and carefully cut out the core and the pips.
2. Slice the apples roughly and put them into the saucepan.
3. Add the sugar and the cold water.
4. Put the saucepan onto the cooker and let the apples cook very slowly over a low heat. It should take about 20 minutes.

Sweetie Pie

You will need 6 ingredients:

1 portion of Sweetie Pie Pastry (see page 86)
1 portion of Apple Filling Station (see page 87)
a little flour
a little caster sugar
some butter
1 egg (or the egg white from the Sweetie Pie
 Pastry recipe mixed with a little milk)

*a flat pie-dish or ovenproof plate (about 25cm
 or 10 inches in diameter), well greased*
a clean work surface
a rolling pin
a knife, a fork and some spoons
a small bowl
a pastry brush
a baking tray
oven gloves and a timer

1. Turn on the oven to 190ºC/375ºF/gas mark 5.
2. Dust the work surface with a little flour and put half of the pastry onto it. Put a little flour onto the rolling pin. Roll out the pastry into a shape, just a little bigger than the dish you are using. Don't press too hard or the pastry will stick. Sprinkle with a little more flour if it does.

3. Roll the pastry up, onto the rolling pin and lift it up, unrolling it onto the dish.
4. Use the knife to cut round the dish to trim off any extra pastry. *Don't worry if the pastry cracks. Just stick it together again as best you can. Use little extra bits of pastry to patch up any holes.*
5. Sprinkle a little sugar onto the bottom of the pastry. Spread out the cooked apples.
6. Put a small blob of butter on top of the apples.
7. Break the egg into the small bowl and beat it with the fork. Brush the beaten egg around the outside edge of the pastry. Keep a bit of egg to brush on the top of the pie.
8. Roll out the rest of the pastry. Roll it up onto the rolling pin again and lift it on top of the pie. Unroll it over the apples, to cover the pie. *Patch up any cracked bits again.*
9. Press the sides of the pastry down all the way around with your fingers to seal the edges.
10. Brush the top of the pie with a little beaten egg.
11. Put the pie onto a baking tray and, using your oven gloves, put it onto the middle shelf of the oven.
12. Set the timer for 40 minutes.
13. When the pie is cooked it will be golden brown and crispy on top. If it doesn't look like this pop it back into the oven for another 5 minutes or so.
14. Sprinkle the top of the Sweetie Pie with a little extra caster sugar.

JUST AS EASY PEASY

• Fill the pie with any cooked fruit that you like. Always taste the fruit to make sure that it is sweet enough. Try plums, blackberries or pears. Or you could fill the pie with Christmas mincemeat.

Sweet Pizza

First you will need 4 ingredients:

Sweetie Pie Pastry (see page 86) made with
   120g of self-raising flour
   45g of caster sugar
   half an egg yolk (beat the whole egg yolk,
     use half and keep the rest with the egg
     white to brush the pastry with)
   2-3 teaspoons of cold water

For the filling you will need 5 ingredients:

500g of ripe plums or apricots
the rest of the egg from the pastry
3 tablespoons of soft brown sugar
a blob of butter
a little extra flour and sugar

a chopping board
a sharp knife
weighing scales
tablespoons
small bowls and a large mixing bowl
a clean work surface and a rolling pin
a pastry brush
a greased baking tray
oven gloves and a timer

1. Make up the Sweetie Pie Pastry as explained on page 86.
2. Cover it with clingfilm and leave it in the fridge for half an hour.
3. When you are ready, turn on the oven to 200°C/400°F/gas mark 6.
4. Wash the plums or apricots, cut them into quarters. Throw away the stones.
5. Put a little flour onto the clean work surface and the rolling pin.

6. Pat the pastry so it is round and flat. Roll it out into a pizza shape, making the pastry about the thickness of a pencil. Add a little extra flour to the rolling pin if it sticks.
7. Use the rolling pin to roll up the pastry, lift it onto the greased baking tray and unroll it. *Don't worry if the pastry cracks, just push it together again with your fingers.*
8. Beat the rest of the egg yolk and the egg white with a fork. Use the pastry brush to brush a little beaten egg over the bottom of the pastry and sprinkle a tablespoon of soft brown sugar over it.
9. Lay the plums in the middle of the pastry, piling some on top of each other. Leave a gap of about 4cm around the edge of the pastry.
10. Sprinkle the fruit with the remaining soft brown sugar and dot it all over with a few blobs of butter.
11. Now fold the pastry edges in – just like a mud pie – to make a rim. This will catch the fruit and stop the juices from spilling out when the Sweet Pizza cooks.
12. Paint the rest of the egg on the outside pastry-rim edges. Sprinkle them with a little more sugar.
13. Using your oven gloves, put the baking tray onto the middle shelf of the oven. Set the timer for 30 minutes. The Sweet Pizza is cooked when the pastry is crisp and golden and the fruit is nicely juicy.
14. Let the pastry cool a little before you share it with friends.

JUST AS EASY PEASY

• Clean about 600g of rhubarb by washing it in cold water. Put the rhubarb into a pot with 3 tablespoons of caster sugar and cook it slowly for about 15 minutes. When it has cooled, drain off the juices, check that it is sweet enough (if not, add a little more caster sugar) and use it as a filling in the Sweet Pizza.

Easy Freezy

Hang on! Before you begin:

- Easy Peasy means **being prepared**. Get everything ready before you start cooking.

- Easy Peasy means **being accurate**. Make very sure that you have the **correct ingredients** and that they are weighed out exactly as in the recipe.

- Easy Peasy means laying all the ingredients out in the **order that they are listed** and counting to make sure that you have everything. Work your way along the ingredients as the recipe tells you and then you won't miss anything out.

- If the recipe tells you to do something you don't understand, look back at the sections on '**How to be a Brilliant Baker**' (see page 9) and '**Bits and Pieces**' (see page 20).

- Remember to **take care** when using sharp knives and always use oven gloves when taking things in and out of the oven.

- Remember to **turn off the oven or cooker** when you have finished cooking.

- Easy Peasy Baking means leaving the kitchen **clean and tidy**.

Chilly Banana

You will need 3 ingredients:

2 bananas
300g of frozen raspberries (not defrosted)
some cream, whipped if you like

weighing scales
a liquidiser with a lid
a chopping board and a knife
a spatula
2 small glasses

1. Pop the raspberries into the liquidiser.
2. Peel and chop the bananas. Add them too.
3. Put the lid on and whiz for a few minutes.
4. Using the spatula, scrape the mixture out of the liquidiser and divide it between the glasses.
5. Add a blob of cream before sharing.

JUST as easy freezy

• You can make this with any frozen soft berries; maybe strawberries or blackberries or mixed soft fruits.

Square Sticks

Make flavoured ice squares in ice-cube trays. Fill them with any juice flavours you like. Put a couple of toothpicks in and freeze them for a sunny day.

You will need 3 ingredients:

a punnet of strawberries or raspberries
   (about 225g)
a little icing sugar
a mug of orange juice

a liquidiser with a lid
a sieve
a big mixing bowl
a wooden spoon
a tablespoon
a mug
an ice-cube tray
toothpicks

1. Rinse the soft fruit. Twist off the stalks and throw away any mouldy fruit.
2. Put the rinsed fruit into the liquidiser, put the lid on and whiz for a few minutes.
3. Balance the sieve over the mixing bowl. Tip the soft fruit into the sieve and press the fruit with the wooden spoon. The juices will drip into the bowl, leaving the seeds behind in the sieve. Remember to scrape any extra juice from underneath the sieve. Throw the seeds away.
4. Add a teaspoon or so of icing sugar to the juice to sweeten it. Taste it to check. Add the mug of orange juice and stir everything.
5. Divide the mixture into the ice-cube tray. Put it into the freezer.
6. After an hour or so, stick the toothpicks into the cubes to make square lollies.
These lollies can be kept refrigerated for 2-3 weeks. When you want to take some out, dip the tray in a little hot water to loosen the ice and then use the toothpicks to pull the Square Sticks free.

JUST AS EASY PEASY

• Squeeze fresh orange juice and pour it into the ice-cube tray.
• Make cola cubes by filling the ice-cube tray with cola. Yum!

Hot Chocolate Sauce

You will need 3 ingredients:

100g of chocolate (any kind you like)
2 tablespoons of butter
8 tablespoons of double cream

a large mixing bowl
a small saucepan
tablespoons

1. Break the chocolate into small pieces and put it into the mixing bowl. Leave it somewhere warm to start to melt, maybe near a radiator or the cooker.
2. Put the butter and the cream into the small saucepan and heat them slowly until they start to boil. *Never leave cream or milk heating because it can rise up the sides of the saucepan and boil over very easily.*
3. As soon as the cream mixture is boiling pour it over the chocolate and stir until the chocolate has all melted and the sauce is smooth.
4. This is especially wonderful, brilliant and yummily fantastic poured hot over ice-cream or sundaes.

Sunny Sundae

You will need 10 ingredients:

1 ball of raspberry sorbet
1 ball of mango or peach ice-cream
1 ball of vanilla ice-cream
4 strawberries
half a mango
1 banana
1 kiwi fruit
ready-to-squirt cream
1 teaspoon of Raspberry Jem (see page 112)
   or raspberry jam (if you want)
1 chocolate flake

a chopping board
a sharp knife
a long glass
an ice-cream scoop
a large bowl

1. You can use any fruit and flavours that you like. Mix tinned and fresh fruit if you can't find all the fresh fruit in season. Make sure that all the fruit is sweet and ripe. Mango, pineapple, kiwi, peaches and nectarines all work well.
2. Prepare the fruit and throw away all the skins and pips. Cut the fruit into small bite-sized pieces.
3. Pile the ice-cream and fruits in layers in the tall glass.
4. Put some slices of kiwi fruit on top and add a squirt of cream.
5. If you like, add a splash of Raspberry Jem to finish off the flavour with a blast of sweetness.
6. Stick the chocolate flake in the top.

Slush

You will need 3 ingredients:

about 6 oranges or 500ml of fresh orange juice
half a lemon (to squeeze a teaspoon of juice)
1-2 tablespoons of caster sugar

a sharp knife
a chopping board
a lemon squeezer
a teaspoon, a tablespoon and a fork
a plastic ice-cream tub with a lid

1. With the sharp knife, cut the oranges in half on the chopping board and squeeze out all the juice. Pour the juice into the plastic tub.
2. Squeeze the lemon and add a teaspoon of juice to the tub.
3. Add 1-2 tablespoons of sugar. Taste the mixture. Don't make it too sweet.
4. Put the lid on the plastic tub and put it into the freezer.
5. After an hour or so, take the tub out and stir the slush with a fork. This breaks up the ice crystals.
6. Put the tub back into the freezer for another couple of hours.
7. Eat the slush when it's really hot and sunny.

Lemon Lush

You will need 3 ingredients:

60g of caster sugar
250ml of cold water
enough lemons to make 250ml of lemon juice
  about 4 or 5

weighing scales
a saucepan
a measuring jug
a sharp knife
a chopping board
a lemon squeezer
a small sieve
a plastic ice-cream tub with a lid

1. Put the sugar and water into the saucepan.
2. Turn on the heat and very slowly bring the mixture to the boil. Let it boil quickly for 5 minutes.
3. Turn off the heat. Let the syrup cool.
4. Cut the lemons and squeeze out the juice. Sieve the juice into the measuring jug.
5. Add the lemon juice to the syrup and pour it all into the plastic tub. Put the lid on.
6. Put the tub into the freezer. After an hour or so, bring the tub out and whisk everything together with the fork to break up the ice crystals.
7. Eat Lemon Lush on a nice hot sunny day or even in the rain!

Chocolate Chip Ice-Cream Sandwich

For each sandwich you will need 2 ingredients:

2 chocolate chip cookies
some vanilla ice-cream

a plate
an ice-cream scoop
a mug of hot water

1. Put a chocolate chip cookie onto the plate.
2. Dip the ice-cream scoop into the mug of hot water. Then use it to scoop out a big ball of vanilla ice-cream.
3. Pop the ice-cream on top of the cookie. Press it down a little.
4. Press the second cookie on top of the ice-cream to make the sandwich.

JUST aS EASY PEASY

• You can make an ice-cream sandwich with ordinary digestive biscuits and chocolate chip ice-cream.

Banana Shake

You will need 3 ingredients:

half a banana
3 balls of vanilla ice-cream
a mug of full-fat milk, well chilled

a liquidiser with a lid
a knife and a chopping board
an ice-cream scoop
a glass, a long spoon and a straw

1. Peel and slice the banana.
2. Put the banana and 2 balls of the ice-cream into the liquidiser.
3. Add the milk.
4. Put the lid on the liquidiser and whiz for a few minutes.
5. Pour the shake into a tall glass and add the extra ball of ice-cream so it floats on top. Serve with a long spoon and a thick straw.

JUST as easy peasy

• Double the quantities to make another one for a friend.
• Try chocolate and banana shake with 2 balls of chocolate ice-cream and half a banana.
• Try a strawberry shake with 2 balls of strawberry ice-cream, 6 strawberries and a mug of milk.

Trifle Tower

You will need 7 ingredients:

a packet of strawberry jelly
6 trifle sponges
250ml of cold Yellow Belly Custard (see page 80)
1 banana
1 small tin of pineapple pieces or 4 slices of
    fresh pineapple
1 kiwi fruit
1 small carton of cream, whipped (see page 32)

a measuring jug
small mixing bowls
a chopping board
a knife
a vegetable peeler
4 long glasses
a tin opener
a tablespoon

1. First make the jelly. Dissolve the cubes in a mug of water in a small saucepan. Pour the jelly into a measuring jug and make the volume up to 550ml with cold water. (Check the instructions on the packet to see this is the right amount of water.) Cover the jelly and as soon as it is cool, put it into the fridge to set.
2. When the jelly is set, start to make up the Trifle Tower.
3. Prepare all the fruit, cutting it into small slices.
4. Break the trifle sponges in half. Wedge 3 halves into the bottom of each glass.
5. Open the tin of pineapple. Tip the pineapple and the juice into the bowl. (Throw away the tin!) Pour a tablespoon or so of the pineapple juice onto each sponge to soften them.
6. Put slices of banana, kiwi fruit and pineapple into each glass. Keep 4 slices of kiwi fruit for decoration.
7. Now put some jelly into each glass. Top this with a tablespoon or so of the cold custard.
8. Finish each Trifle Tower with some whipped cream and a slice of kiwi.
9. Chill them in the fridge until you want to eat them.

JUST AS EASY PEASY

• You can make trifle with any combination of fruit that you like. Leave out anything that you don't like. You decide!

Not so Easy Peasy – But you can do it

Hang on! Before you begin:

- Easy Peasy means **being prepared**. Get everything ready before you start cooking.

- Easy Peasy means **being accurate**. Make very sure that you have the **correct ingredients** and that they are weighed out exactly as in the recipe.

- Easy Peasy means laying all the ingredients out in the **order that they are listed** and counting to make sure that you have everything. Work your way along the ingredients as the recipe tells you and then you won't miss anything out.

- If the recipe tells you to do something you don't understand, look back at the sections on '**How to be a Brilliant Baker**' (see page 9) and '**Bits and Pieces**' (see page 20).

- Remember to **take care** when using sharp knives and always use oven gloves when taking things in and out of the oven.

- Remember to **turn off the oven or cooker** when you have finished cooking.

- Easy Peasy Baking means leaving the kitchen **clean and tidy**.

Pick Me Up

You will need 6 ingredients:

10 trifle sponges, savoiardi or boudoir biscuits
1 small tin of pineapple pieces
250g of mascarpone
115g of single cream
2 tablespoons of icing sugar
2 teaspoons of cocoa powder

weighing scales
a tin opener
a flat, shallow bowl or soup plate for dipping
  the biscuits into
small bowls
teaspoons and tablespoons
a hand-held electric blender
a sieve
a flat, shallow glass serving dish or some small
  glass dishes
a spatula

1. Open the tin of pineapple and drain the juice into the shallow bowl or soup plate.
2. Dip the sponges (or biscuits) into the pineapple juice, just enough to let each one soak up a little of the juice.
3. Put each sponge onto the bottom of the serving dish. Break them up to make them fit snugly in one layer.
4. Put the pineapple pieces on top of the sponges.
5. Put the mascarpone, cream and sugar into the mixing bowl. Use the hand-held electric blender to whisk everything together until it is quite fluffy.
6. Use the spatula to spread the cream over the sponges and pineapple.
7. Sift the cocoa powder over the cream to give a lovely chocolaty dusting.
8. Leave the Pick Me Up pudding in the fridge for half an hour or so before eating it.

JUST AS EASY PEASY

• You can use any tin of fruit that you like. I love stoned cherries.
• You can use pineapple juice from a carton to dip the biscuits in and use slices of banana as the fruit layer.
• Adults usually like this pudding flavoured with coffee. Make a cup of very strong coffee with 2-3 teaspoons of instant coffee in a cup. Use this to dip the biscuits in, instead of the pineapple juice. Layer the cream mixture on top.

Pixie's Burps

You will need 5 ingredients:

75g of strong plain flour
50g of cold butter
1 teaspoon of caster sugar
125ml of cold water
2 eggs

weighing scales
a measuring jug
a sieve
small bowls and a large mixing bowl
teaspoons
a knife
a saucepan
a fork and a small bowl
a wooden spoon
a greased baking tray
oven gloves and a timer
a skewer
a spatula
a wire cooling rack

1. Turn on the oven to 220°C/425°F/gas mark 7.
2. Sift the flour into the bowl.
3. Cut the cold butter into small cubes and put it into the saucepan with the sugar and the cold water.
4. Turn on the heat and slowly let the butter melt.
5. Turn the heat up and as soon as the water is boiling, tip all the flour into it, making sure not to splash or burn yourself.

6. Turn off the heat, and stir the mixture with the wooden spoon until it makes a solid-looking ball. This takes quite a bit of effort so don't give up.
7. Break the eggs into the small bowl and beat them with the fork.
8. Now, add the eggs a little at a time to the dough and, using the wooden spoon, beat the dough until the paste is glossy and smooth. *Don't get a fright. As you add the eggs the mixture will break up and get a bit gloopy. Keep beating and it will form a ball again.*
9. This next step may seem a bit odd, but trust me. Splash the greased baking tray with some water and then just tip any extra water off the tray. This leaves a fine film of water on the tray which helps make steam in the oven while the Pixie's Burps are cooking. This way they will puff up much better.
10. Using 2 teaspoons, put small walnut-sized blobs of paste onto the baking tray, spacing them well apart. You should get about 9 or 10 buns.
11. Using your oven gloves, put the Pixie's Burps onto the highest shelf of the oven. Set the timer for 10 minutes.
12. When the time is up, turn the oven down to 190°C/375°F/gas mark 5 and set the timer for 15 more minutes.
13. When they are cooked the Pixie's Burps should be crisp and golden brown and puffed up inside. Push a skewer into each one to make sure that all the air comes out and they don't go soggy.
14. Use the spatula to put them onto the wire rack to cool.

PIXIE'S BURPS FILLING

• When they are cool, cut the Pixie's Burps open. Fill them with a teaspoonful of Whipped Cream (see page 32) and some chopped soft fruit. Dust them with a little icing sugar (see page 116).

Chocolate Fingers

You will need 3 ingredients:

1 quantity of Pixie's Burps dough (see page 109)
some Whipped Cream (see page 32)
some Hot Chocolate Sauce (see page 97)

a tablespoon and a teaspoon
a greased baking tray splashed with water (see
  Pixie's Burps step 9)
oven gloves and a timer
a wire cooling rack

1. Turn on the oven to 220ºC/425ºF/gas mark 7.
2. Make the Pixie's Burps dough following the recipe from step 2 up to step 9.
3. Use the tablespoon and the teaspoon to put long, finger-shaped blobs of dough on the baking tray, spacing them well apart. They should be about the size of a small chocolate biscuit, 4cm long and 1cm wide.
4. Cook them in the same way as the Pixie's Burps. Follow step 11 onwards.
5. While they are cooling, whip some cream and make the Hot Chocolate Sauce. When the fingers are cooled, slit them sideways. Fill each one with 2 or 3 teaspoons of whipped cream and pour some chocolate sauce over them.
6. Leave them to chill in the fridge for half an hour or so before eating them. I usually can't wait!

Raspberry Jem

This sauce gets very hot and splashes when it cooks. Ask an adult to help you.

You will need 3 ingredients:

500g of raspberries
1 lemon
500g of granulated sugar

a sieve
weighing scales
small bowls
a sharp knife and a chopping board
a lemon squeezer
a large heavy-bottomed saucepan
a long-handled wooden spoon
a timer
a ladle
2 clean jam jars with lids

1. Rinse and check the raspberries. Throw away any that are mouldy. Put them into the sieve and shake them to get rid of any water.

2. Weigh out 500g of raspberries and tip them into the pot.

3. Cut the lemon in half and squeeze the juice. Add the sugar and the lemon juice to the pot with the raspberries. Stir everything together. Turn on the heat. Slowly, slowly let the mixture heat up so that the sugar dissolves and disappears before the sauce starts to boil. *You will know that all the sugar has dissolved if the mixture no longer sounds gritty when you stir it with the long-handled wooden spoon.*

4. Turn the heat up to high. Set the timer for 5 minutes. Let the sauce boil very fast.

5. When the time is up, turn the heat off and let the Raspberry Jem cool a little before using the ladle to put it into the jars.

6. Cover the jars with the lids and when they are completely cold, wipe away any sticky bits on the outside.

7. This is very fresh, soft jam-like sauce. Keep it in the fridge. Use it for toast, cakes, Granny's Scones (see page 57), and Squidgy Snow Cake (see page 114). My favourite way to eat it is to pour it while it is still quite hot over strawberry ice-cream.

Snow white and Red Rose

You will need 4 ingredients:

2 egg whites
115g of caster sugar
some Whipped Cream (see page 32)
a few strawberries to decorate

weighing scales
a large clean and dry mixing bowl
a hand-held electric blender
tablespoons
a spatula
a greased baking tray lined with non-stick baking
   parchment
oven-gloves and a timer
a fish-slice

1. Turn on the oven to 140°C/275°F/gas mark 1.
2. Separate the egg whites from the egg yolks
(see page 14). Make absolutely sure that there
aren't any small specks of yellow yolk left in the
whites or they won't whisk.
3. Put the egg whites into the clean dry mixing bowl
and use the blender to whisk them until they start
to look like white fluffy snow.
4. Now slowly add the sugar and whisk it all together
until the mixture doubles in size. It will get quite
glossy and stiff. When you take the blender out
of the mixture *(switch it off first!)* it will stick to
the beaters in spikes, just like the tops of snow-
capped mountains.
5. Use 2 tablespoons to put small mounds of
mixture onto the greased and lined baking tray,
spacing them so that they don't touch.
6. Using your oven-gloves, put the baking tray on the
bottom shelf of the oven. Set the timer for 1 hour.
7. When the time is up, turn off the oven. If you can,
it's best to leave the meringues in the oven until the
next day. This makes them dry out and keeps them
crisp. If you can't wait, just let them cool out of the
oven.
8. When they are completely cool use the fish-slice
to ease the meringues off the paper.
9. Serve them by sandwiching two meringues
together with a little whipped cream, topped with
a strawberry.
10. You can store these without any filling in a tight-
lidded tin. They will last about 2-3 weeks.

Squidgy Snow Cake

You will need 4 ingredients:

3 egg whites
175g of caster sugar
1 teaspoon of cornflour
1 teaspoon of white vinegar

weighing scales
small bowls and a large clean and dry mixing bowl
a hand-held electric blender
teaspoons and tablespoons
a greased and lined baking tray
a skewer
oven gloves and a timer
a fish-slice
serving plates

1. Turn on the oven to 140°C/275°F/gas mark 1.
2. Put the egg whites into the large clean mixing bowl. Make very sure that there are no specks of yellow yolk in the whites or they will not whisk.
3. Use the hand-held electric blender to whisk the egg whites until they are light and fluffy.
4. Add the caster sugar and keep whisking until the mixture looks like the snow peaks on a mountain.
5. Add the teaspoon of cornflour and the vinegar and whisk them in.
6. Divide the mixture into 6 round dollops onto the greased baking sheet. Press the middle down a little with the back of a spoon and use the skewer to flip the edges of the mixture up at the sides to make a nice nest shape.
7. Using your oven gloves, put the tray onto the bottom shelf of the oven. Set the timer for an hour.
8. When the time is up, use your oven gloves to take the tray out of the oven. If the cakes are cooked they will be quite crispy and firm. If they look very soft, pop them back into the oven for another 15 minutes.
9. Leave the Squidgy Snow Cakes to cool completely. Use the fish-slice to transfer them onto plates.
10. This is the fun part. You can fill the Squidgy Snow Cakes with anything you fancy. Try Whipped Cream (see page 32) and Raspberry Jem (see page 112), jelly and soft fruit, ice-cream and Hot Chocolate Sauce (see page 97), or even some Cream Fool (see page 33).
11. You can store the Squidgy Snow Cakes in a tin with a tight-fitting lid (before they are filled with anything). They will last for about 2 weeks.

Icing Dust

Icing dust makes a cake or pudding look really great and it's Easy Peasy!

You will need:

1 tablespoon of icing sugar

a tablespoon
a sieve

1. Put the icing sugar into the sieve.
2. Hold the sieve over the cake or pudding that you want to dust.
3. Gently tap the side of the sieve with your hand. The icing will drizzle down like fine snow over the cake. It looks very posh!

JUST aS EaSY PEaSY

• Use drinking chocolate powder or cocoa powder to make dark dust.

Using a Squirting Bag

You might have a piping bag or squirting bag in your kitchen. If you do, try using it to pipe whipped cream. Get the cream ready first (see page 32). Don't over-whip it or it will get too thick and buttery.

1. Fit a nozzle into the bottom of the bag. Usually this is just pushed down to the bottom of the bag.
2. Fold the top of the bag over to make a hem or cuff. You can then tuck your fingers under this little hem to hold the bag. This stops it slipping all over the place.
3. Use a big spoon in your right hand while you hold the bag with your other hand (or the other way round if you are left-handed). Half fill the bag with whipped cream.
4. Press the air out of the piping bag by moving your hand down from the top, easing the cream towards the nozzle.
5. Balance the bag in your left hand, near the bottom, and use your right hand to squeeze a little at the top. The cream will squirt out of the nozzle. This gets easier with practice.
6. You can use piped cream to decorate cakes or buns or to fill meringues or Chocolate Fingers (see page 110).

Just Chocolate Icing

You will need 4 ingredients:

50g of plain or milk chocolate
2 tablespoons of cold water
15g of butter
2-3 tablespoons of icing sugar

weighing scales
a heat-proof measuring jug
a small saucepan
some cold water
a sieve
a large mixing bowl
a tablespoon
a spatula
a palate knife and a mug of hot water

1. Put the chocolate, the cold water and the butter into the heat-proof measuring jug.
2. Put the jug into a small saucepan. Pour some water into the saucepan, enough to come halfway up the jug on the outside. Put the saucepan onto the cooker and heat it until the water starts to simmer. Lower the heat and let the water bubble gently until the chocolate melts. (Or you could use a microwave to do this. Ask an adult to help.)
3. Sift the icing sugar into the large mixing bowl.
4. When the chocolate mixture has melted, use your oven gloves to lift the jug out of the hot water in the saucepan.
5. Pour the melted chocolate onto the icing sugar.
6. Use a spoon to stir everything together to get a smooth shiny chocolate icing.
7. If the icing is too thick, add an extra teaspoon or so of hot water. If it is too runny add some more sieved icing sugar.
8. Dip the palate knife into the mug of hot water. Then dip this hot knife into the chocolate icing. Spread the chocolate icing over Just Chocolate Cake (see page 118). This way the icing spreads easily and is nice and shiny.

Just Chocolate Cake

You will need 8 ingredients:

3 tablespoons of hot water
1 heaped tablespoon of dark cocoa powder
125g of soft butter or margarine
125g of caster sugar
2 large eggs
125g of self-raising flour
1 teaspoon of baking powder
2 tablespoons of milk

To serve, you will need:

Whipped Cream (see page 32)
Just Chocolate Icing (see page 117)

weighing scales
small bowls and a large mixing bowl
a sieve
teaspoons, tablespoons and a fork
a hand-held electric blender or an electric mixer
a large metal spoon
a spatula
a greased and lined 20cm (8 inch) round baking
  tin, at least 5cm (2 inches) deep
oven gloves and a timer
a skewer
a wire cooling rack
a long sharp knife
a palette knife

1. Turn on the oven to 180ºC/350ºF/gas mark 4.
2. Add 3 tablespoons of hot water to the cocoa powder in a small bowl. Stir to make a paste.
3. Put the soft butter (or margarine) and sugar into the large mixing bowl. Use the hand-held electric blender to beat the mixture until it is pale, creamy and almost doubled in size.
4. Break the eggs into a small bowl and beat them a little with a fork. Add them to the mixture. Add the cocoa paste too and beat everything together.
5. Sift the self-raising flour into the mixture. Add the baking powder. Fold everything together with the large metal spoon. Mix in the milk.

Check that all the ingredients are in the mixture.

6. Use the spatula to scrape the mixture into the greased and lined baking tin.
7. Using your oven gloves, put the tin on the middle shelf of the oven. Set the timer for 35 minutes.
8. When the time is up, use your oven gloves to lift the cake out of the oven. If it is soft and springy to touch in the middle, it is cooked.
9. Put a skewer into the middle of the cake. If it comes out clean, it is cooked. If not, put the cake back into the oven for another 5 minutes.
10. Let the cake cool in the tin a little before turning it out onto the wire cooling rack.
11. When the cake is cool, use the long sharp knife to cut it in half along the middle. Pile whipped cream onto the bottom half and put the other half on top.
12. Make some Just Chocolate Icing and use the palate knife to spread it over the Just Chocolate Cake.

Just Brilliant!

How to Splash Chocolate Mixture all over the Kitchen Ceiling

Getting Ready

It's no use trying to make a cake or some buns with the wrong ingredients or the wrong tin. **Read through the recipe** before you start and get everything laid out and measured in the order that it is listed in the recipe. After that it's Easy Peasy.

Aprons

Well, an old shirt would do. I wear an apron and I look really silly, but I stay clean underneath. You decide! What you don't want are sleeves that have to be pulled up all the time, so wear something with short sleeves.

Chopping Boards

In the kitchen, raw meat and fish can leave **nasty little bugs** on chopping boards. They're not easy to spot unless you have X-ray eyes. So, any chopping for baking should be done on a board that is only used for things like cutting bread or making sandwiches (not a board that has had raw meat or fish on it).

Eggs

It's bad news, but **raw and lightly cooked** eggs can have nasty little bugs in them. It's tough, but, believe me, it's **not safe to lick** the mixture when you're baking if there are raw eggs in it.
Young babies and toddlers, very old people or mums that are pregnant shouldn't eat raw eggs or even meringues.

Hand-held Electric Blender

Using one of these is by far the easiest way **to splash chocolate mixture** all over the kitchen ceiling. Simply take the mixer out of the chocolate mixture while it is still on. Everything will whiz all over the place. So, remember to switch off the mixer **before** you take it out of the mixture. Switching on a liquidiser without the lid on will also give the same effect!

Knives

Sharp knives really are **sharp**. They need to be in order to work well, so be careful not to cut your finger off! Use a knife that's comfortable in your hand. Hold it and the food you're cutting firmly – and it helps if you keep your eyes open. Serrated knives are the ones with the jagged blades. Fruit can get slippy while you cut. Sometimes it's a good idea to push a fork into the fruit and use that to steady it while you cut.

Electricity

You know this, don't you? Electricity and water **don't mix**. So NEVER touch electric things in the kitchen with wet hands. Be extra careful when you use the hand-held electric blender. Don't go near the sink with it, and make sure that you have unplugged it before you wipe it with a clean damp cloth. The beaters can be taken off to be washed separately.

Floors

Untidy and slippy floors are especially dangerous in kitchens. So are banana skins. If you spill something on the floor, **mop it up** and dry the floor right away. You don't want to fall into the cake mixture, do you?

Frozen Foods

Things that are frozen last a lot longer. If you are freezing something, make sure it is completely cold before you put it into the freezer. Once you defrost something you must use it – it can't be **re-frozen**. You might find this hard to believe, but frozen metal containers can be very sticky and can burn your fingers. Use a tea towel to take them out of the freezer.

Wash behind your ears

It's no fun eating something that's been cooked with hands that have last week's **grub under the nails**. Be kind to your friends. Wash your hands (with soap) before you start. It's not a bad idea to fill the sink with soapy water and wash your hands as you go. Baking is a pretty sticky business.

Work Surfaces

Baking makes a bit of a mess, so it's no good having a mess to start with. **Clear a big clean space** and, if necessary, move your brother's football boots if he's dumped them on the work surface! It's probably easier to roll pastry out on a clean work surface rather than a chopping board. Use what you like best.

And finally...

Don't tell anybody, but the best way to get into adults' good books is to leave the kitchen **sparkling**. If you don't want to do it yourself, bribe your wee brother or sister with a promise of a share of the goodies you've just baked. It's amazing, and not everybody knows this: hot soapy water and a clean dish cloth can do wonders when you're cleaning up. And, if everything is put back into the cupboards, you'll know where to find things next time you have the **uncontrollable urge** to do some Easy Peasy Baking.

How to avoid Blood, sweat and Tears in the Kitchen

Cuts

They hurt a lot. Even the little ones hurt and they give you a fright. One of the ways to avoid cutting yourself is to **concentrate** on what you are doing. If you do cut yourself, wash the cut under cold, running water, dry it and put a plaster on. Try not to cry – it affects the amount of salt in your baking! If the cut is a bad one, wrap it up tightly in a clean towel and call an adult.

Sweat

Not the kind you get when the kitchen's too hot. It's the kind you'll be worked into if you don't clear as you go. If you tidy up from the start, putting away the bags of ingredients after you have weighed out what you need, then things won't be half as bad at the end. You'll have time for a quick whiz round the garden and a bit of telly while the cake cooks. Always use clean cloths, by the way, unless you want to deploy a whole **army of bugs** over your work surface.

No sweat!

Burns

There are endless ways to burn yourself in the kitchen. And there are good ways to avoid burns:

- Never leave the handle of a saucepan on the cooker sticking out.
- Never leave a cooking spoon in the saucepan while something is cooking.
- Always use oven gloves to handle hot things.
- Always have somewhere heatproof and safe cleared in advance, ready to put things down when you take them out of the oven.
- Don't be too **independent**. Where a recipe asks you to check with an adult, **please, please, please** do so. It's too painful to get a bad burn just out of stubbornness.
- If you do burn yourself, turn off the heat and pour **very cold** water over the burn for at least 10 minutes. It may feel like you're freezing to death but it will take the sting out of the burn. Most kitchen burns are OK after that. Don't put a plaster over it. If your burn is serious and really, really hurts, call an adult and get medical help.

Heat

Heat is hot. Be careful. You'll be amazed at the heat that can come bursting out of a hot oven when you open the door. Even the steam from a saucepan can be very hot, especially if it has a tight lid and liquid boiling away inside. Don't get too close to the gas burner when you switch on the cooker. Sometimes there's a delay between turning on the gas and it actually lighting. When that happens there's often a burst of **flame** that can come as a bit of a shock. It is the same principle with the oven. If you have heated it before you make the recipe, watch out when you open the door. Apart from the temperature, it'll steam up your glasses if you wear them. Some cooked things are **ever so much hotter** than even boiling water: things like jam, toffee and oil. Be extra careful and keep well away from them.

Distractions

Dogs, cats, **fast swimming goldfish** and babies are all pretty much unwelcome in hot, busy kitchens. In fact, so is anything or anyone which takes your mind off the job.

P.S.

Oh, and by the way, if you're wondering what
happened to the higgeldy-piggeldy house, it's
empty now. The children have all grown up
and live in higgeldy-piggeldy houses of their own.

Some of them even have higgeldy-piggeldy children,
who, as far as I know, still get up in the middle
of the night and cook fantabulous, extraordinary,
scrumptious midnight feasts as well.

Index